Disaster Preparedness

Disaster Preparedness

Heather Havrilesky

RIVERHEAD BOOKS

a member of Penguin Group (USA) Inc.

New York

2010

RIVERHEAD BOOKS
Published by the Penguin Group
Penguin Group (USA) Inc., 375 Hudson Street, New York, New York 10014, USA •
Penguin Group (Canada), 90 Eglinton Avenue East, Suite 700, Toronto, Ontario M4P 2Y3,
Canada (a division of Pearson Penguin Canada Inc.) • Penguin Books Ltd, 80 Strand, London
WC2R 0RL, England • Penguin Ireland, 25 St Stephen's Green, Dublin 2, Ireland (a division of
Penguin Books Ltd) • Penguin Group (Australia), 250 Camberwell Road, Camberwell, Victoria
3124, Australia (a division of Pearson Australia Group Pty Ltd) • Penguin Books India Pvt Ltd,
11 Community Centre, Panchsheel Park, New Delhi–110 017, India • Penguin Group (NZ),
67 Apollo Drive, Rosedale, North Shore 0632, New Zealand (a division of Pearson
New Zealand Ltd) • Penguin Books (South Africa) (Pty) Ltd, 24 Sturdee Avenue,
Rosebank, Johannesburg 2196, South Africa

Penguin Books Ltd, Registered Offices: 80 Strand, London WC2R 0RL, England

The author gratefully acknowledges permission to quote from the following:

"Pierre." Words and music by Carole King and Maurice Sendak. © 1975 Colgems-EMI Music Inc. and Elorac
Music, Inc. All rights controlled and administered by Colgems-EMI Music Inc. All rights reserved. International copyright secured. Used by permission. Reprinted by permission of Hal Leonard Corporation.

"This Jesus Must Die" from *Jesus Christ Superstar*. Words by Tim Rice. Music by Andrew Lloyd Webber.
Copyright © 1969, 1970 Universal/MCA Music Ltd. Copyright renewed. All rights for the U.S. and
Canada controlled and administered by Universal Music Corp. All rights reserved. Used by permission.
Reprinted by permission of Hal Leonard Corporation.

"Toads" by Philip Larkin, from *The Less Deceived*, published by The Marvell Press in England and
Australia.

Library of Congress Cataloging-in-Publication Data
Havrilesky, Heather.
Disaster preparedness / Heather Havrilesky.
p. cm.
ISBN 978-1-59448-768-2
1. Pessimism.   2. Emergency management.   I. Title.
BF698.35.P49H38   2010   2010003043
818'.609—dc22
[B]

Printed in the United States of America
1   3   5   7   9   10   8   6   4   2

BOOK DESIGN BY AMANDA DEWEY

FOR MY MOTHER,
who still bakes a damn good cherry pie

Contents

Disaster Preparedness

Introduction

Growing up during the '70s, I found it hard to avoid the specter of disaster. On every movie screen, airplanes plummeted to the ground, earthquakes toppled huge cities, and monster sharks ripped teenagers to bloody bits. But more disturbing than the catastrophes themselves was the utter lack of foresight demonstrated by the adults in each harrowing scene. As meteors hurtled toward Earth and gigantic dinosaurs crushed cars under their feet, grown adults either ran screaming or stood in confused clusters, gasping and shrugging over what was to be done.

Why wasn't there a plan? I always wondered. How could so many adults stare blankly at each other as everything went to hell?

Once I asked my mom what we would do if a meteor crashed into the house. "The chances of that happening are *very* slim," she told me. But it *could* happen, I told her, and I needed to know what to do if it did.

"Well, we wouldn't be able to *do* anything. The house would explode in flames and we'd all be incinerated in seconds." My mom thought about that for a second. "But that's not a terrible

way to die, compared to getting really sick or maimed and having to be wheeled around or kept alive with tubes forever."

My mom was about as bad at reassuring a little kid that the
world was a safe place as anyone could be. She would start out on
the right track, but then give up almost immediately, exhausted
by the effort of forming optimistic lies she didn't believe. "*Some
people think that there's a heaven,*" she'd start out saying when
some pet or distant relative died and I wanted to know what
would happen to them, "but I've always thought that was wishful
thinking, honestly." Or: "The chance of lightning striking the
house is something like a million to one . . . but, then again, it *did*
strike that tree in the side yard last year, didn't it? And we *are* on
a hill, covered by tall trees."

Despite my mom's acceptance of our potential annihilation,
I knew there had to be a way out of any bad situation. In every
disaster movie ever made, no matter what cataclysmic scenario
was unfolding, there was *always* a way to avoid death, if you had
a plan. *But you had to have a plan.* So my sister Laura and I decided
that it was up to us to form a strategy for handling each potential
emergency, from natural disasters to nuclear war to unlikely
crime scenarios like dognapping.

In case of a tornado, we concluded that we should grab the
pets and as many cans of mini-ravioli as we could carry and hide
in the basement. If there was a nuclear attack, we resolved to seal
all the windows with aluminum foil and duct tape and take
showers every two hours. In case of a flood, we agreed that the
best move was to inflate the little raft in the garage and haul it up
to the roof so we'd be safe until the water rose very high.

Our plans weren't always logical. In case our house caught on fire, for example, I was supposed to grab my teddy bear and our dog, Madge, stuff them into a pillow, and throw them out the window. My sister was in charge of rescuing the cat and the Star Wars action figures. Next, we'd throw one of our mattresses out the window, and then jump out the window and land on the mattress.

This wasn't the soundest approach, considering that there was a perfectly good fire-escape ladder in the hall closet upstairs. But we had never *used* that ladder, so we weren't sure how it worked. In fact, my mom would mention at least once or twice a year that we *really* needed to test that fire-escape ladder. Just spotting the box in the closet gave me a sinking feeling inside. A picture on the front of it showed a voluptuous woman in a tiny nightgown, lightly stepping down a chain ladder amid a raging fire. She bore an uncanny resemblance to Farrah Fawcett, and not only looked calm but had a slight smile on her face as red and orange flames licked at the hem of her nightie.

This image of poise in the face of adversity struck me as utterly fantastical. My sister and I knew better than to put our faith in such a traditional, accepted means of rescue. The people who did that in the movies—exited calmly with the crowd, trusted the lifeboats, followed the posted signs—were always the ones to perish first. Only a small band of survivors willing to plot out their own escape route and battle their way through untold mishaps had any hope of making it out alive.

We never ran our emergency drills by my mom, who might've liked to know that if there was a fire, her two daughters would die struggling to shove a mattress out the window. But it seemed more reassuring to have a plan that our parents weren't in on, maybe because we didn't always trust their judgment under duress. Childhood is a wild, unpredictable ride whether your parents are good drivers or not, and our parents alternated between puttering along cautiously and careening all over the road, shouting at each other as they swerved and fishtailed through uncharted territory.

The stakes always felt unnervingly high. But even though we could crash at any second, we still enjoyed the scenery together. Some spirit of recklessness and longing attracted my parents to each other, and we were enlisted in their strange bond. We echoed their hotheaded tirades, we matched their loud, cackling laughter, we soaked in their ambient melancholy. They were young and opinionated and stubborn and overwhelmed by violent emotions; we were caught in their undertow. Even my earliest memories are vibrant and sweet and vaguely menacing: a loud fight, a silly song, a made-up game, an hour of sullen silence, a walk among the fireflies at twilight. We loved our king and queen, but their kingdom was an untamed and volatile place.

And then there was the larger world outside, with its fearmongering teachers and anxious bullies, its fickle boys and sadistic cheerleading coaches and bad bosses and disapproving friends and indifferent but watchful strangers. The claustrophobia of our odd little gang of five gave way to a wider universe that was even more bewildering. Maybe we grew up during a particularly reckless decade, when people drove fast in cars without functioning seat belts and let their dogs run free through the neighborhood as a pack, chasing cars and terrorizing cats. Or maybe my mom and dad were particularly invested in making us aware of just how cruel and unforgiving the world could be. Their blustery jokes and self-assured swagger belied a deeply pessimistic, dark view, in which people were assumed to be selfish or unjust or careless or deluded or all of the above.

But this isn't the story of my parents' failures, or how the world beat me up or let me down. Instead, I chart my trajectory from expecting way too much—from my parents, from the world, from myself—to then, later, as a coping strategy, expecting way too little. Like most children, I was unaware that my path to disillusionment was a thoroughly trampled one: I put my faith in a loving and all-powerful God, and then one day suspected that we were all alone on our tiny sphere, sailing through an enormous universe, fragile and unprotected. I believed that my parents could keep me from everything bad in the world, and then one day I recognized that they were relatively powerless, whether they were grappling with a potential catastrophe or their own shortcomings.

When the world began to feel unsafe to me, I looked for reassurance from two parents who were unwilling to tell me fairy tales about how it would all turn out just fine. I suppose they thought it would be a disservice to me, to feed me comforting myths. Or maybe they couldn't stand to shield their kids from ugliness that they themselves were never sheltered from as children. It was better to be tough and resilient, like they were, than to be overprotected and naive. Only fools allowed themselves to be vulnerable to the unknowns. Only chumps hoped for the best. It was far better to expect the worst, even if you weren't remotely prepared for it.

I decided that I *would* be prepared. But once you've lugged all of the crates of food and water and gas masks and bedding and matches and batteries you need into your bunker, once you've rechecked the locks and tested the Coleman stove and turned on the shortwave radio, there's nothing left to do but wait. And when you're huddling in the dark, waiting for the first bombs to hit, the tiniest mosquito starts to sound like an incoming missile.

Better to walk out into the sweet night air, where falling bombs look just like shooting stars. Even as you watch them fall, your destruction starts to feel far less certain.

1

Cousins

When I was a kid, my brother and sister and I made up an alternative version of Clue that we called "Cousins." Instead of trying to solve a murder, players would receive murder assignments: Kill Colonel Mustard, in the Billiard Room, with the candlestick. This felt far more immediate and exciting than detective work. Rather than passively collecting evidence, you were the protagonist: You had to find the candlestick, kidnap Colonel Mustard (sometimes he was another player), and drag him into the Billiard Room to be killed. Afterward, you had to escape without being stopped by the police, and you had to make sure there weren't any witnesses.

This is where the cousins came in. A herd of faceless nobodies pilfered from Sorry, cousins would migrate together through the hallways and rooms of the Clue board based on the spin of a compass lifted from our Bermuda Triangle game. If a cousin was in the room when you committed your murder, you'd have to track him down and kill him, too.

While we loved debating the parameters and rules ("Colonel Mustard should be able to grab a weapon to fight you by rolling the dice, Risk style!"), the game itself was sort of tedious. It proved to be exceedingly difficult to murder someone and escape without notice. The unruly herd of cousins would inevitably become lodged in the hallways and doorways, trapping players in the Ballroom or the Lounge with no way of exiting. Even when you did end up in the right place with the right weapon, there might be four or five cousins in the room, all of whom would have to be chased down and murdered before they got to the police.

Looking back, the notion of a game of murder doesn't bother me. But why were they "cousins"? Why not "witnesses" or "bystanders" or "strangers"? Apparently it seemed perfectly natural to my brother and sister and me that the pesky mob that would sooner or later be our downfall would be made up of blood relatives.

AROUND THE TIME my parents stopped making the slightest effort to hide their distaste for each other, we started taking long family vacations in the car each summer. This is the perverse logic of two people caught in a crumbling marriage: Instead of spending as little time together as possible, they vow to spend *more* time together, thinking that they might reignite some lost spark through the purgatory of enforced contact. Maybe they imagined that, side by side all day long in the front seat of their '76 Impala, their three kids prattling happily in the backseat, the open fields of the Midwest a blur of wheat and sunshine rushing by their windows, suddenly they'd find the love that had been largely obscured since their first year of marriage. Minutes together were sure to end in bickering and angry outbursts. But hours together, in the family sedan? Those held more promise.

Not surprisingly, these trips always felt like high-stakes affairs, chilling adventures in which our entire lives were on the line. My parents didn't help matters much by reminding us, repeatedly, that the family's ability to have *fun* absolutely depended on the good behavior and cooperation of each of us—five stubborn individuals who were neither well-behaved nor particularly cooperative.

But as we backed out of the driveway, our hopes were always high. There were chicken-salad sandwiches packed in the cooler, there were bright summer clothes and bathing suits stuffed in our duffel bags, fueling our hopes of a Holiday Inn with a big pool out back. The extra-large Rand McNally road atlas was passed back and forth between the three kids, so we could size up the road ahead. States, states, so many states! Tennessee was in our sights, then we'd get to Missouri and Kansas and Colorado, states so exotic, each with its own plucky flag, its own state flower and state bird and state animal and curious license plate. We looked forward to the strange rest stops with new sorts of bathroom faucets that swiveled like video-game joysticks, we anticipated the endless hikes through every national park and state park along the way (my father loved steep eight-mile trails, and we were expected to trek like tireless Sherpas by age five). We could hardly wait to visit all those souvenir shops, filled with snow globes and little pewter charms the shape of each state, where we'd walk around and point to things and beg, but rarely wind up with more than a sticker. We were excited about the quiz competitions my dad hosted as he drove—"Who said, 'Don't fire until you see the whites of their eyes!'?" I could never remember the right answers, but I was the youngest, so I was comfortable with being proclaimed the dumbest by my older siblings. Being the dumbest afforded me a certain freedom of expression, the freedom that comes from lowered expectations.

An adventure lay ahead, we knew that. But even on shorter trips to see our grandparents in Pennsylvania or Illinois, after a few hours on the road, with so many miles of monotonous freeway stretched out in front of us, Eric and Laura and I would descend into a claustrophobic nightmare of shoving, whining, and tears, punctuated by barked threats from the front seat. Often the chaos began with us kids, but our squabbles were minor compared with those of our parents, who, after even a little time in the car together, could barely exchange small bits of information without snapping at each other or growing quiet and staring out the window for several hours without speaking.

At home, we could always run off to our rooms or build a fort out of couch cushions or go outside and hop on our bicycles and ride to the park for some extended meditative seesawing. But in the car, there was no relief. After a week or so on the road together, the cranks and pulleys of our already creaky machine ground to a halt. All of the unspoken resentments and nagging hurts we'd accumulated over the years would lodge in the gears, throwing sparks and smoke.

One summer it all came to a head in the middle of Kansas, when my mom sat down at a picnic table at the edge of a big, grassy rest stop and announced that she wouldn't be getting back into the car with my dad. This was the grand gesture of a woman who knew she was trapped. If it were possible to leave my father, if we weren't Catholic, if she didn't feel certain that she'd ruin all of our lives in leaving, if this weren't years before all of our friends' parents started getting divorced, she might not have wasted her time and energy on such a dramatic display. She might've sat quietly in the front seat and mapped out her exit strategy.

But leaving wasn't an option. So, cornered by her circumstances, a demonstration was in order. A rest stop in the middle of Kansas seemed like a suitable setting for showily demanding an end to the senseless torture of her failing marriage.

As I stared through the backseat window at my mom on that picnic bench, arms folded, wind sweeping across the rolling hills and whipping her hair around her face, I didn't think she was just being dramatic. I figured she would stay there for as long as it took for us to drive away without her. I imagined that she'd find a place to rent in some nearby town and then spend the rest of her life there, without us. Maybe she would be happier without us. Maybe she would find work on a sunflower farm and she'd make new friends and she'd sometimes have to crouch in the basement with her neighbors, just as they did in *The Wizard of Oz* when big tornadoes blew through.

Just as I was starting to consider joining my mom at that picnic table, so that I could live in Kansas, too, and crouch in the basement with the neighbors when big tornadoes blew through (which sounded sort of exciting, actually), my dad stepped on the gas and we all went hurtling off down the freeway, leaving my mom behind, getting smaller and smaller in the rear window.

We yelled at my dad to turn around, but he didn't listen. He told us to shut up and he didn't look back for at least a quarter of a mile. He was determined to punish my mom for her melodrama with his own theatrical demonstration of indifference—you know, sort of like the thing you do with toddlers, when they don't want to leave the playground?

Finally, though, my dad turned the car around and pulled up by the picnic table and my mom begrudgingly got in and we all learned an important lesson that day about commitment and marriage and sticking together as a family, no matter what. Namely, it was pure hell.

MY MOTHER DIDN'T SIMPLY decide to draw a line in the sand that day in Kansas, on a whim. No, she looked around at the wind gusting across the rolling, grassy hills, she took in the huge oak trees on the hillsides, their dappled shady spots buffeting and churning, she studied the lonely picnic table lingering at the edge of the rest stop, and she knew this was the place. Like a seasoned location scout, she'd found the perfect setting for her next scene.

My parents weren't just argumentative or combative. Those words don't do justice to the breathtaking vision and electrifying dynamism of their collaborations. They were passionate artists who knew just how to construct explosive but nuanced scenes, rich with heartbreaking details.

Since they recognized the importance of imagery, a wide se-lection of props was used to reflect the emotions raging to the surface, the disappointment and anger that, once you ran out of words like "motherfucker," really had nowhere else to go. The wildest emotions require an adequate vessel—an object, something not too big and not too small, preferably something that can break into lots of little pieces.

There is *the sandwich* that soars across the room in a slow-motion arc and lands with a satisfying splat at the protagonist's feet. There is *the shattered window* that explodes in a glorious burst of light and sound when struck at full force with a bare fist, a spectacular embodiment of marital discord sprung straight from the pages of a John Updike novel.

But the best prop of all has to be *the chocolate cake* that is made just for Daddy's birthday. Mommy bakes it from scratch and ices it as Daddy and the kids are eating dinner. Jazz plays from the stereo in the living room, those endless clarinets that the children recognize are clarinets because *both* of them, Mommy and Daddy, played the clarinet in their high school marching bands, just another little detail of their backstory that superglued them together like unhappy fingers. Suddenly Daddy mutters something disparaging about the meal. Yes, you can see from that dissatisfied look on his face that he's searching for a target, a way to liven things up a little. Mommy snaps at him—she's not in the mood for a show, but Daddy won't back down. So Mommy finally takes her cue. She is standing next to us, birthday cake in hand. But there are no candles! Aren't we going to sing "Happy Birthday"? With her glare fixed on Daddy, Mommy drops the cake. It hits the floor and implodes in a big chocolatey mess. Chocolate crumbs and shards of white china plate scatter across the floor. Now the children are drawn into focus, staring down at the collapsed cake and the pieces of good white china. (*God,* they're natural. Where did you *find* them?) Their faces tell us that this might be the saddest scene they've ever performed. Bravo! Bra-*vo*!

ONCE THE CURTAIN DROPS, we stand up, like patrons at a movie theater, and look for the nearest lighted exit. I walk, zombie-like, up the stairs to my room, and quietly shut the door, and sit on my bed and stare at my poster of a cat trying to catch a gold-fish in a bowl.

No one will knock on my door for a couple of hours, at least. I have plenty of time to feel sick and replay the scene in my mind. I feel sorry for my mom, because I know she'll be cleaning up those pieces of plate and chocolate crumbs off the floor, question-ing her latest performance. She'll wonder if it's really art, after all. Maybe they aren't artists, maybe they're just assholes.

I feel sorry for my brother, in his room alone, probably con-vincing himself that it's no big deal. I feel sorry for my sister, even though I hate her a lot of the time, for being so mean about everything. I feel sorry for my dad, his birthday is ruined. This will always be the ruined birthday, the year he turned thirty-six, the year he ruined his own birthday, that sorry son of a bitch, the year his bitch wife ruined his birthday.

I feel sorry for all of us, in our little house, each in our own room, staring at the wall.

I THINK I SPENT most of my third-grade year at my friend Melanie's house. She had eight older sisters and brothers, and her house had all of the toys our mom wouldn't buy for us: Sit 'n Spin, Hungry Hungry Hippos, Don't Break the Ice, Operation, toys that my mom always said we'd get sick of in two seconds, toys that she said were designed for kids without imaginations. But when I went to Melanie's house, I was happy to sit and spin, without imagination. I was happy to get dizzy in the midst of the bedlam created by so many kids, the oldest of whom was what my mother referred to hyperbolically as a "juvenile delinquent," which he proved in part by putting firecrackers in Melanie's Barbie Dream House and blowing it to smithereens. At least there weren't any Barbies inside at the time.

I was happy to sit, utterly devoid of original thoughts, and make the hungry hippos bite each other. I was happy in this imaginationless pocket of existence, where there were no performers around, sketching out new scenes and acts, writing and rewriting their endings to suit their moods that day. Instead, Melanie's mom made ham sandwiches with yellow mustard on Wonder bread. We never ate this way at home. She poured Pepsi into big Looney Tunes glasses and set out huge bowls of Ruffles potato chips. We watched cartoons while we ate. Nothing was left to the dangers of the imagination.

Melanie's room was filled with posters of little girls with pointy heads and wispy hair, little girls who held hands and smiled. The posters said things like *Sharing is caring* and *A friend is always there when you need her.* My mother would never buy posters with such saccharine words on them. My mother didn't actually believe that sharing was caring or that a friend was always there when you needed her. But Melanie was my friend, and when I looked at those posters, I knew that maybe they were a little tacky and smarmy, but those rainbows and smiles secretly made sense to me.

At night, Melanie and I stayed up very late talking—Melanie was a good talker, she could talk more than anyone I knew. One night, out of nowhere, when the glowing red numbers on the radio alarm clock said 2:46, Melanie suddenly got very serious and told me that sometimes she thought about killing herself. It was dark in her room and the happy little wispy girls were staring at me with their big saucer eyes, watching me and smiling. They knew exactly why Melanie would want to kill herself. Those smug little sharing, caring girls knew there was a reason, but they weren't telling.

I didn't understand, so I asked Melanie why, and she couldn't tell me. We were quiet for a while and I thought about how Melanie's dad was hardly ever around, and how Melanie's mom rarely talked to him even when he *was* there. Melanie's mom always seemed a little depressed, and her gray hair made her look about ten years older than her husband. I asked Melanie again why—gently, I didn't want to make her feel worse about it—and she said she didn't know, she just felt like it would be better not to have to deal with anything. It would all be over, and maybe that would be nice.

In the dark I wished I was back at home, not in Melanie's scary room, in the dark, in a house full of big kids and little kids and tons of toys and two parents who rarely spoke to each other, haunting different rooms, mumbling to no one in particular. I wanted to be back in my house, where we were always making up stupid games or getting quizzed on something or being harassed or teased or pinched or scolded, even if we were all in our rooms, feeling terrible, alone, everyone was *there*, maybe some-one ended up turning over the Monopoly board and bursting into tears, maybe my parents were yelling, but we were all still there, no one was missing, and no one was wandering around like a ghost, spreading yellow mustard on white bread without a word while that coyote fell off a cliff with a splat for the hun-dredth time in a row.

The next day when I got in the car with my mom to go home, I sunk into the front seat and sighed deeply and rolled down the window. The trees along the highway seemed greener than the day before, and a choir of cicadas sang their buggy "Hallelujah" chorus as we sped by. As we pulled in the driveway, my mom turned to me and said, with a tone of finality, "Home again, home again, jiggety-jig."

MY JUNIOR YEAR in high school, long after my parents divorced and the spirited performances ended, my sister and brother moved away to college and my mom and I were finally alone together—just like we would've been in Kansas if I had gotten out of the car and my dad had driven away with my brother and sister inside and never come back. Finally, we could live like two friends, not family. We were each going to do whatever we liked, we would eat out whenever we felt like it, and we were never going to fight for any reason. We were two people exhausted by the last eighteen years of chaos, we were longing for a little peace and quiet. There would be no heaviness, only the casual fun of two friends who talk in reassuring, light voices, without telling each other everything.

But that fall, my grandmother started to forget things. She started ordering things from catalogues, and cramming them into the attic, and then ordering more stuff. My aunt asked her what year it was, and she looked at a dime in her pocket: *1968,* she said. We drove up to Chicago and cleaned all of the junk out of her house and sold it, and she came to live with us.

I didn't want my grandmother living with us. Even so, I felt bad for her. To leave behind your house and drive south, why? Why go live with your daughter and a granddaughter you hardly even recognize half the time? Where are the bags of Styrofoam balls and fake purple feathers you were going to use to make beautiful bird puppets? Where are the metal orange-juice lids you saved to use as feet that go clickety-clack? Where are your rubber bands and your pills and your old blue bottles and your secrets? A woman who had many secrets, from her flair for storytelling to her six-pack of beer in the vegetable bin of the fridge, suddenly is reduced to sitting on her bed in a room in her daughter's house, wondering where the hell she is, wondering when she can go home.

That's when I realized that, no matter where I went, even if I lived alone, my family would always follow me. And if they needed something from me, I wouldn't be capable of denying them whatever they needed. There was no escape, then, and there would never be any escape. There will always be lots of cousins around, and grandmothers and sisters-in-law and nephews and aunts and fathers-in-law and uncles. They would *all* be there, gumming up the works and just generally making life difficult. Even when things were good, chances are a cousin was about to wander in and ruin everything.

My grandmother messed up our plan. But even though she exasperated my mom by dipping her lasagna in her water glass at an Italian restaurant or going on long walks with the dog and then sitting on a curb somewhere, lost, until someone called the number on the humiliating bracelet on her wrist, I saw how deeply she belonged to my mom and my mom belonged to her. If my mother indulged herself that day in Kansas, pretending that she could simply sit still and let us keep barreling westward without her, it was precisely because she knew she would never have that option. She could never leave us; we were chained to her like a trail of clumsy prisoners, stumbling a few steps behind her wherever she went. Even if the recklessness of abandoning her family lurked at the edges of her vision, even if it was perversely reassuring to think she could just take off without further notice, even if it was tempting to imagine that it could all be over, and maybe that would be nice, the truth was clear. We were a family, crammed into the same room forever, one or another clogging up the doorway and making a quick exit impossible.

Age and distance and hundreds of little and big tragedies later, the anguish of those performances by my parents is still with me, along with the excitement and tension of those long car trips together. But I also remember how my dad got us to list all of the state capitals, and he sang cowboy songs about cool, clear water and tumbling tumbleweeds. I remember how my mom sat in the shade with me at the Grand Canyon when I was tired, talking about skittering lizards and why the rocks there were such a bright shade of red. I remember how my grandmother rode in the front seat, with her purse in her lap, happily reading every single road sign out loud—"Cornwallis Road!" "Hardee's hand . . . no, *ham* biscuits!"—as my mom mumbled her feigned interest. When you're not glued to other people, you don't bother to feign interest or sit with them when they're tired or sing them cowboy songs to make the miles pass by more quickly.

When it comes to family, there is no escape. The beauty— and the nightmare—of family is how well they know you after so long, and how deeply you belong to each other. There is no easy exit. There are witnesses, and they remember everything.

2

Fear Itself

In January of my fifth-grade year, my social studies teacher, Mrs. Taylor, reminded us that the Iran Hostage Crisis had gone on for more than 427 days. Sure, we probably already knew that . . . but did we truly understand the dire nature of the situation? Did we really *get* that this international standoff could result in widespread bloodshed and mayhem?

"You know what this could mean, don't you, folks?" she stage-whispered to a room full of rapt ten-year-olds. We didn't really *want* to know, but we could see that we had no choice—Mrs. Taylor's eyes were bulging out of their sockets in that way that told us she was determined to terrify us.

"This could mean World War . . ." Instead of saying the number, she flashed three fingers at us, then walked around the room so everyone could get a good look at that ominous number. She wanted to give us plenty of time to let the impending apocalypse sink in.

"World War Three, folks! World War *Three!*" We all gasped

in unison, forming a squeamish Greek chorus to her alarming narrative. Would bombs start falling on us at any minute? Would we have to hide in the basement with our pets, eating canned green beans, until the air-raid sirens quieted down? Would our fathers be drafted? Would we have to do our parts by quitting school to work in the steel mills, churning out battleships and tanks like Rosie the Riveter?

Just as our imaginations were starting to make a third world war sound vaguely exciting and worthwhile, Mrs. Taylor interrupted us again, suspecting that we needed the precise drawbacks of a bloody global conflict spelled out for us.

"Remember, *this* time we're not the only ones who have nuclear weapons, folks. And the Russians—who are *good friends* with Iran—have bombs that can flatten an entire city the size of Durham *in an instant!*" She let that one sink in, eyes bulging. Did the woman never blink? "World War Three will make World Wars One and Two look like . . . *child's play!*" Child's play? Didn't millions of people die during World War II?

At the time, my parents were getting divorced. This wasn't a common occurrence at a Catholic school in the '70s, so all of the teachers were informed that they should keep an eye on my sister and brother and me, to look for signs of depression or suicidal ideation. We didn't know they'd been warned that we were living in a broken home until my mom told us later, but it explained a lot. Every now and then, a teacher would pull one of us aside and ask, with a meaningful look, if *everything was okay.*

Clearly, everything was *not* okay, not just in our house but in the wider world outside. Not that I shouldn't have known by then to take Mrs. Taylor's charming anecdotes with a grain of salt. She took great pleasure in striking terror in the hearts of her students. Naturally her extracurricular fearmongering had nothing whatsoever to do with her role as our social studies teacher. She'd frighten us with just about anything she could think of: deadly viruses, natural disasters, bridge collapses, train wrecks. She sought out gruesome stories of death and destruction just to savor every little horrifying detail. She must've told herself she was preparing us for the real world, when really, she was just giving us all anxiety disorders.

One day Mrs. Taylor spent a solid twenty minutes of class time telling us the story of a little boy she knew—a friend of a friend's kid—who had been having these recurring headaches. But (cue the bulging eyes) *no one knew why!* His mom and dad took him to the doctor, but the doctor said there was nothing wrong with him, so he went home. A few days later, though, he woke up in the middle of the night, *screaming in agony!* His parents took him to the emergency room, and after a much more thorough examination, it turned out that . . . the little boy *actually had maggots eating his eyeball from the inside out!*

Oh, sweet Jesus, no! The entire class squeezed their eyes shut and moaned.

Yes, it's true, she told us. Apparently the little boy had been *petting a dog,* or maybe *a dog licked him on the eye,* and the dog's tongue maybe had some *eggs* on it, and the eggs hatched, and well, *thank God* they went to the hospital when they did! He lost his vision in one eye, but if they'd waited any longer, he might've gone totally blind, or the maggots could've moved to his brain. *Who knows?*

Now, it was one thing to fear World War III. That was

something big that would affect everyone on the planet. Once the bombs started falling, we were all toast, sure, but at least we were all in it together.

But eyeball-eating maggots? That was a whole different matter. Why, you so much as pet a stray dog, or let a dog lick you on the face, and you could wake up in the middle of the night *with maggots eating your brains out!* You could go blind or die and *no one would ever even know what was wrong with you!* This was the sort of fear that a fragile ten-year-old could really sink her teeth into.

Mrs. Taylor was so effective at her work of instilling paranoia in us that, by the time the hostage crisis actually ended, it hardly mattered. I was still sure that World War III could break out at any second, just as I was sure that I might be crushed under the rubble of a badly designed building or catch a deadly flu or wake up with a suspicious headache behind one of my eyes. Nothing was in my control—nothing was in *anyone's* control. The whole globe's population was helpless against the whims of Mother Nature, a handful of arrogant architects, a few deeply disturbed world leaders, and one tiny pregnant insect.

And did Mrs. Taylor announce to the entire class that the hostages were returning home? Did we have a little party to celebrate the resolution of this extended national nightmare?

No. Where was the fun in that? She probably told us about a mudslide or an overturned school bus instead.

BUT MRS. TAYLOR was just a product of the times. Plenty of parents and teachers in the '70s made very little attempt to shield kids from the harsh realities of life. They'd been raised by the so-called greatest generation, stoics who tended to idealize toughness and grit and stick-to-itiveness, but who often had an unfortunate habit of drinking themselves into a stupor and beating the hell out of their wives and children. Without adequate therapy, those children—our parents and teachers—had to survive by telling themselves some version of the story that their parents fed them, that being verbally and physically abused *only made them stronger.* It wasn't so bad, not really, that's *just how things were back then.*

But how would kids today be half as resilient? these parents and teachers asked themselves and each other. These kids had it so easy. They seemed so carefree. They'd get eaten alive! Better to take them by their little collars and shake some sense into them, before they wandered out into the world, unawares, only to be taken down by the nefarious forces—pedophiles and serial killers and rabid dogs and ayatollahs—that lurked around every bend.

So when, not long after my parents' divorce was finalized, my mother's checking account came up $200 short and one of her checks was mysteriously unaccounted for, she told me about it. I was ten years old, but even then I remember thinking that my mom probably wrote a check for $200 that she simply forgot to record in her checkbook.

To my mom, such a mistake was inconceivable. She was a *math major in college.* This was her first personal checking account *ever.* She was keeping *meticulous* records. There was no *way* she could have made a mistake! So instead, she walked into the last place she wrote a check—Whitewater World, the outdoor store where she'd rented a tent so we could camp at the beach—and asked the bearded hippie behind the counter if maybe, just maybe, he'd found one of her checks lying around and if he had, if he had happened to, you know, need some extra cash at the time.

She very politely accused the man of check fraud, in other words. And not surprisingly, this man, who quite possibly smelled of Dr. Bronner's magic soap, who was more than likely wearing socks with sandals at that very moment, this gentle, Bambi-loving, herb-growing, river-kayaking feminist, told my mother, "Take your shit and get the hell out of here." (By "your shit" my mom thought he might've meant my sister, Laura, who went into the store with her that day, unaware of her intention to confront a suspected criminal.)

That proved it, as far as my mom was concerned. This wolf in hippie shearling had *obviously* stolen money from her—*and he still had her checking account number, too!* He could steal *more* money from her, if he really wanted to. Plus, now he knew that my mom *was on to him!*

Maybe the check was only the beginning, now that the guy had a personal grudge against my mother. "I don't know what that guy is capable of," she said. "He could come by one day and *blow up the house* for all I know."

Having spent a sizable proportion of my time on earth watching Wile E. Coyote try to blow the Road Runner to smithereens, this sounded completely plausible to me. So instead of concluding that my mother was suffering from paranoid thought patterns in the wake of taking on the enormous responsibilities of single motherhood, I spent the next two years of my life worrying that a tent-renting, socks-and-sandals-wearing hippie was going to stick a bunch of dynamite around the foundation of our house and then hide in the bushes with a detonator and blow us to little bits. It wasn't clear what he would accomplish by this act, of course, but this was 1981. People did crazy things when they wanted to get Jodie Foster's attention, let alone when they thought some watchdog citizen was going to blow the lid off their hippie check-fraud ring, up until now cleverly concealed behind a fussy outdoor-equipment store.

Come to think of it, though, who in Durham, North Carolina, was kayaking on rivers, anyway? Most of the people we knew spent their weekends sucking on Orange Juliuses at the mall, not trudging through the swampy, buggy hinterlands, lugging around enormous boats and paddles. There was obviously something suspicious about this guy's need to grow a scraggly beard and be alone in the wild at a time when everyone else was out shopping for Members Only jackets. My mom was probably right: Our house could explode into flames at any second!

This fear was far more personal than the fear of nuclear war, or of egg-laying insects. Nuclear war didn't discriminate, and tiny insects remained faultless. But seething, enraged hippies who forged checks and told middle-aged moms to "Get your shit and get the hell out of here," these sorts of men were more frightening than almost anything. Men like that were worse than John Hinckley, Jr., the Shah of Iran, and a few dozen Turkish gunmen combined, because they knew my mother and they hated her, *and* her "shit"—meaning us, her children! These infuriated bohemians hated all of us, the whole family! Who even knew why? They had stockpiles of dynamite in their back rooms, where the tents and kayaks should go! They were out of their bearded, patchouli-scented, river-loving minds!

Fear is a funny thing. If you fear one very concrete, easy-to-imagine thing, that awakens the fearful part of your brain, and your mind is transformed into a fertile, hospitable place for *all other fears*.

Thus, no sooner had I begun plotting out a quick escape path in case I happened to notice that the house was about to explode (Luke Skywalker always made a hasty escape *before* stuff exploded, didn't he?) than I began to take on other fears, too. When darkness fell each night, a host of robbers and murderers and child molesters flocked to the bushes outside our house, waiting for their moment. I couldn't see them, but in my mind, they were always there.

And how would we protect ourselves against them? My dad could scare off most intruders, with his barrel chest and his bellowing voice, but he had moved out almost a year earlier. He wouldn't be any help to us at all, across town in a condo full of new furniture and with a copper Datsun 280ZX out front and a rotating cast of younger girlfriends, girlfriends who smiled and cooed at me like I was a toddler while I studied their sprayed hair and carefully applied makeup and concluded that they were too boring for my dad. It was so unfair. The girlfriends and the 280ZX would be safe from intruders, but the rest of us were goners.

There was only my brother, who had just hit the slouching, ineffectual, "Shaggy" stage of puberty, and my sister, who was certainly scary but also got scared easily, and our little dog, Madge, who hid under the bed during thunderstorms.

My mom could be pretty fierce, particularly when you left your socks in the living room before a book-group party. I'd seen her fly into a rage plenty of times, occasionally while simultaneously balancing on a ten-foot ladder and cleaning pine needles out of our gutters. Her anger was efficient, effective, and fearless. But she seemed a little panicked at the moment. She was less tightly wound in some ways, finally alone with her kids, with no husband to provoke her, but she was a little more jittery than usual, too, as if this fragile, newfound independence might be stolen from her at any second.

BUT EVEN BACK when my parents were still together, not only didn't they shield us from the dangers of the real world, but, like Mrs. Taylor, they paraded those dangers in our faces. My mom talked casually and at great length about grisly freeway accidents, or recounted how this or that child of a friend had been killed, dismembered, or disfigured, using only a few common, seemingly harmless household items. My father took me to see *Earthquake*, and shook the back of my seat whenever the ground started shaking in the movie.

As soon as the 1978 remake of *Invasion of the Body Snatchers* came out, my dad took all three of us kids to see it. I had no idea that this was a legendarily frightening movie, a movie about murderous aliens who emerge, slimy and horrific, from exotic houseplants. The aliens form exact replicas of real people; you can't tell the aliens from the humans. When an alien spots a human, it points and emits a terrible screeching sound, to warn the other aliens that there's an imposter among them.

Fair enough, I thought, *I'll just wait for the human race to prevail over this extraterrestrial scourge.* But after fighting a losing battle against the pod people and seeing his entire city, including most of his friends, transformed into soulless demons, our hero is walking down the street, trying not to be noticed by the pod people, when he's spotted by a woman who may be *his last surviving human friend*. She rushes over to greet him, and our hero . . . points and screeches! He's a pod person! Oh, noooooo! Roll credits.

I was eight years old. I'd never seen a movie with an unhappy ending before, let alone an unhappy ending that involves aliens taking over the planet. I couldn't *believe* that was the ending. I just sat there, appalled, as the credits rolled. I felt dizzy and confused. My dad laughed all the way out of the theater.

When I mentioned to my dad a few months later that taking an eight-year-old to see such a scary movie isn't that nice, he just smiled and chuckled. So I told him that I'd been having terrible, wake-up-screaming nightmares ever since we saw it. This made him imitate the pod person at the very end of the movie, pointing and screeching.

My dad had a highly developed sense of humor.

BUT EVEN ALIENS weren't as bad as angry hippies—enraged, river-riding, homemade-explosive-wielding hippies with big grudges to bear. Alien invasions seemed like the naive fears of an eight-year-old mind, by comparison, not nearly as sophisticated and realistic as pissed-off check-forgers or robbers or child molesters or rapists or other criminal types who I could imagine lurking in the bushes outside our house.

It was particularly easy to picture someone breaking in through my bedroom window, since my dad had placed the torso of a mannequin out there a few years earlier to scare the hell out of us. You know, *just for kicks*.

Luckily, my brother and my mom and I had all walked in while my dad was dressing the mannequin in a plaid shirt and a black skier's cap, so there was only one person left to frighten: my sister. This was the perverse nature of being raised by wolves: When you weren't personally being terrorized, you gleefully engaged in terrorizing anyone else you could. So, as my brother and I giggled through our hands, my dad set up the mannequin on the ledge outside my window, then called Laura.

"Go open the window in your room—it's hot in here and we need some airflow."

Laura was immediately suspicious. "Why don't *you* do it?"

"Because I'm relaxing here. Go on!"

"No! *You* go do it!" she snapped.

My mom made her voice threatening. "Laura, go open the window like Daddy told you!" Oh ha ha, we all thought. This was going to be good.

Laura had hardly touched the window at all when she started screaming, screaming like the world was ending, screaming like she not only saw a scary faceless man in a plaid shirt outside the window, but also spotted a figure just beyond him, an angry hippie crouching in the bushes with a detonator. Laura screamed and ran into my parents' bedroom, where she found her parents and big brother and little sister, all laughing hysterically. She was furious.

To her credit, my mom *did* get a guilty look on her face—like, for just a minute she wondered if it was really appropriate, from a childhood-development, trust-building perspective, to play terrifying practical jokes on your already jumpy and somewhat neurotic kids. She'd have to look that up in *I'm OK—You're OK* later.

Unfortunately, the mannequin not only gave me a chance to witness just how horrifying it would be to have a murdering intruder perched just outside our window at night, but it also provided a firsthand demonstration of how the members of my family would react in an emergency situation: My sister would fall to pieces, and my parents would laugh their asses off. Then they'd tell my sister to stop being so melodramatic and they'd send us all to bed.

THE TORTURE TRICKLED DOWN in my family, from my parents to my siblings to me. Each time my parents left the house, my brother and sister found creative ways to torment me. One afternoon when I was eight, I was sitting outside with the dog and they came up behind me and threw a pillowcase over my head. Then they dragged me upstairs, locked me in the closet, and snickered as I yelled and then cried and begged to be let out.

Once they finally opened the door, I told them I was going to tell on them and they were going to get in huge trouble (unlikely). Then they both disappeared. I spread a blanket on the ground outside, and set out a bunch of my stuffed animals to have a picnic with me. I was determined to have a good time by myself, no matter what.

A few minutes later, my sister appeared with a dish towel hanging over her arm and a menu written in crayon.

"Welcome to Le Restaurant. Here is le menu. What would you like?"

I was still mad, but I couldn't resist. I looked down at le menu. There was a wide assortment of delightful lunch items listed. They must've really been scared of getting in trouble.

"Um . . . I'll have the fruit salad."

"I am so sorry, madame, we are out of that," my sister said lightly. "Might I suggest the tomato fizz?"

"No. I'll have the tuna sandwich."

"Oh, I am sorry, madame. We just served our last tuna sandwich. We are all out. You might very much enjoy the tomato fizz, though."

This continued for several minutes, with me ordering different things and my sister indicating that Le Restaurant was out of that item, until finally, the only thing left on the menu was the tomato fizz.

"I guess . . . I'll have the tomato fizz," I told my sister.

"Very good choice," she said primly, then disappeared. A few minutes later, she reappeared with a fancy cocktail glass filled with club soda and V8 mixed together. The glass was resting on a dish that had a Flintstones vitamin as a garnish.

I set the glass and the dish down and ate the vitamin. I had to admire their ingenuity in spite of myself, in spite of the fact that the joke was on me. The joke was on me, sure, but they were also making it up to me, trying to soften me up after their abuses. With tomato juice, and club soda, and a kid's vitamin. It was a weak effort, but I drank the tomato fizz anyway. This was a gift, somehow, even though it was a joke. This was how they indulged me, even as they laughed at me, drinking their nasty drink, from behind the back door.

That was the odd line that we walked, together, which our parents taught us to walk. We filled each other with fear and anger, then made jokes and laughed together, to soften the blows, or laughed at each other's expense. Sometimes it was hard to tell the difference.

And when my parents got back home and I told them what had happened, my mom scolded my brother and sister mildly, but she and my dad almost seemed pleased that the mice had gotten up to such lively fun while the cats were away.

AND DID MY MOTHER tell us when she located the lost check, and realized her accounting error? Did we have a little party to celebrate the resolution of this extended family nightmare?

No. Where was the fun in that?

As it turned out, it was only my personal nightmare. Years later, when I asked my mom if she was really fearful that the Whitewater World guy would come after us and blow up the house, she laughed.

"Blow up the house? Who said that?"

"You said he might come by and blow up the house, for all you knew."

"What a weird thing to say. I don't think I ever said that."

I knew she'd said *exactly* that, of course. I couldn't get that sentence out of my head for two whole years. But the event that haunted me was relatively insignificant to her at the time. She had never *really* considered the Whitewater guy a threat. She admitted that she was a little paranoid in the wake of her divorce, and maybe she'd felt ashamed of confronting the guy, so she implied that he might be dangerous. She'd wanted to march into that store to prove that she could stick up for herself. She wanted to reassure herself that, as a single mother, she could handle any problems that came up, head-on. She wanted to make sure she could keep us all safe.

Maybe even Mrs. Taylor was trying to keep us safe, in her own twisted way. If we were aware of the dangers out there, maybe we could find some way to avoid them. And maybe my father wanted us to be immune, to encounter scary movies and cruel practical jokes with skepticism or mild amusement. Maybe they were all trying to toughen us up by scaring the crap out of us.

My father dragged his own father home from the bar on Friday nights. My mother hid in her room when her mother drank and cursed and threw things. They wanted us to be different, to encounter terrifying circumstances with aloof laughter, or even outright scorn. They wanted us to be chided and shamed until we were protected, armed against the world. The ideal was to watch, skeptical, unmoved, from a safe distance.

But this also gave them an excuse not to rein in their own temperamental outbursts. We suffered in the name of toughness, and grew increasingly fearful in the name of fearlessness. We were to laugh in the face of pod people and enraged hippies. But in so doing, we would have to keep our expectations in check, and set our sights low. We would never be hopeful, because hope was naive. The hopeful got hurt. Towns filled with hopeful people were killed in an instant. We knew better than to hope. We would skip the good things on the menu and just order the tomato fizz.

3

Faculty Wives

Can she bake a cherry pie, Billy Boy, Billy Boy?
Can she bake a cherry pie, charming Billy?

My mom sang this song every time she baked a cherry pie. She sang it with an ironic, lilting voice that seemed to mock whoever would pose such a question. It was the voice of some prying, busybody neighbor, the sort of old-fashioned woman who would dare to suggest that a woman's worth could be measured by something wrapped up in a crust and baked in an oven.

But while my mother sang, her hands moved confidently and swiftly, rolling out the dough with bold, strong strokes, lifting the top crust over the filling in one smooth motion, then bending the decorative edges together expertly. *She* could bake a cherry pie, goddamn it. She could bake a cherry pie *and* she could paint the bathroom ceiling *and* she could sew Halloween costumes *and* she could build a bed frame *and* she could recognize every constellation in the nighttime sky *and* she could solve complicated differential equations *and* she could do a lot of other things, too.

My mother was capable, and she was proud of it. She was capable and she would've made a suitable wife to any man. Both sides of that equation were important. That crooning busybody voice may have jeered at the notion of a woman's worth, from a man's perspective, but my mother wanted to be admired on her own terms *and* on a man's terms.

On this particular afternoon, my mother was baking a cherry pie because her friends Christine and Joan were coming over. Christine and Joan would briefly greet us by the door, sigh over how much we'd all grown, then they would disappear with my mother into the dining room, doors closing behind them. In a few minutes, the smell of coffee and cherry pie and cigarettes would drift out from under the door, along with the sound of three women talking intensely. Now and then, laughter would rise up from the room in a three-part chorus, with my mom's deep cackling *ha-ha-ha*, Christine's convulsive, gasping laugh that almost sounded like an asthma attack, and Joan's high-pitched, singsongy peals of pure hysteria. Hands slapped down on my mom's butcher-block table, hard. Laughter like that always meant that my mom and her two friends were talking about their jackass husbands.

The three women had met at an academic function years ago, their husbands young professors in different departments at the local university. They had quickly fallen into step over the odd nature of having landed in their current supporting roles in life.

These intelligent, independent women, full of ideas, capable, strong, proud of their abilities, found themselves holding down the home front, raising the children, and throwing the occasional department function. They were faculty wives.

When they talked, sometimes it was hard to decide which of their husbands was the biggest jackass of all. Christine's husband, a biologist, was extremely passive and detached. He withdrew from Christine, he withdrew from his two sons, Craig and Adam, and no amount of urging him to get involved seemed to change a thing. The man was so invisible, so half there, that I can't picture him at all. He was the disembodied voice coming from the La-Z-Boy chair in front of the TV set in Christine's house.

Joan's husband, Harry, was very involved with his kids but also a little irritating. He was a fun dad, goofy and engaged, but he could also be kind of whiny. Even though he was a psychology professor, prone to pontificating at length about this or that, it was hard to take him seriously: that wavering, nasal voice, the slightly insecure way he held himself. In the company of my own father's growling arrogance, Harry always seemed a little wilted and defensive.

But I think Christine and Joan agreed, even if my mother didn't, that my father was the worst of them. My mother's stories—what little I could make out of them, sitting on the other side of the dining room door, straining to hear—always seemed to elicit the most cries of "That *bastard*!" (Christine) or "That *asshole*!" (Joan) or, from my mother herself, "The *son of a bitch*!" My father was pushing the envelope of what it meant to be a jackass husband. He was an innovator—a true radical. Hearing their disbelief at my dad's latest antics, I felt perversely proud that my dad was the bold-est jackass of them all.

But every movement needs a radical edge to push it forward. Just as faculty wives needed tales of deliciously nasty behavior by their academically respected, long-winded blowhard hus-bands to illustrate the particular domestic traps they found them-selves ensnared in, so, too, did your average jackass husband need his own signature method of lashing out in order to live on the bleeding edge of jackassery, thereby pushing back against a gag-gle of overly critical wives, women who'd taken on traditional roles that didn't quite dovetail with their ideas of themselves or with the changing times.

Whenever I asked my mother why she married my father, she didn't have much of an explanation, romantic or pragmatic or otherwise. "I knew I would never be bored," she'd say simply, as if boredom were a fate far worse than death, a million times worse than living with someone who was careless and insensitive and made you clench your fist in anger a few times a day. It *was* true: My father was anything but boring.

But mostly, she explained, it was a timing thing: She was a senior in college. She fell in love, and got married. That's just what you did back then.

"Sounds like musical chairs to me. The music ends, and you grab whatever chair isn't taken," I told her.

"It *was* sort of like that," she said quietly.

Those Friday afternoons were a brief respite from her domes-tic incarceration. In our dining room, with both doors closed, she and her two friends worked themselves into a state of cathartic, caffeine-, nicotine-, and sugar-fueled, slightly tragic laughter.

. . .

CHRISTINE OR JOAN would sometimes bring their kids along with them when they came over. Christine's sons Craig and Adam were a year older and a year younger than my older brother, Eric. They were both bigger and gruffer than Eric, and they always seemed to be running in circles around the house, yelling. At first, the three of them brought their teddy bears everywhere they went. The teddy bears would go flying by the windows outside as the boys ran around the house, shouting to each other. The teddy bears got treated to rides on the swings in the backyard. The teddy bears would go for adventures on the golf course down the hill. We have pictures of all of us, in the back of Christine's VW van, the boys all holding their teddy bears next to their faces like they were all part of the same club.

But a few years later, the bears disappeared. I asked Eric where the bears went, and he told me that Craig and Adam had burned theirs in the fireplace. I was shocked.

"Why did they do that?" I wanted to know.

"I guess they figured they'd outgrown them," my mom answered for him, as if that were a perfectly reasonable explanation for setting fire to your lifelong best friend.

My mom had set fire to plenty of friendships over the years. College roommates or next-door neighbors were mentioned here and there, but generally she seemed to end friendships that threatened to become too time-consuming or involved. My mom was self-sufficient, after all. Even after we were all in school and she was home alone for most of the day, she had plenty to do. Tulip bulbs needed planting, leaves needed raking, the kitchen ceiling needed to be plastered and then repainted. She wasn't one for mom groups or afternoon coffee with neighbors or PTA meetings. She joined the babysitting co-op for practical reasons; she joined a book group so that once a month, she could spend a few hours discussing books with other women who . . . well, some of them were a real piece of work, but at least they were reasonably smart and read a lot. But my mother's best, most trusted friends were Christine and Joan.

My mom and Christine never fought, and my mom and Joan had only one fight that I can remember. Joan had left her son Sam, who was two years younger than I, in my mom's care one afternoon. The two of us were playing in the sandbox in our backyard, and Sam, who was three at the time, kept throwing sand in my eyes. My mom told him to stop. Sam threw sand again. My mom told him that if he threw sand one more time, he was going to get a spanking.

This was a natural progression in our house: If you made it clear that you were being bad just for the sake of causing a stir, you were treading on thin ice. My mom hardly even had to mention that you might get spanked; usually a look was enough to make you move on to some subtler form of aggression, like ripping up grass for no reason or scolding the dog or hiding behind the couch and "bombing" any sibling who walked by with wooden blocks. Every once in a blue moon, though, it was tempting to believe that a spanking might just be worth a little more bad behavior.

After the spanking, however, your cost-benefit analysis of being bad was typically readjusted to accommodate reality. My mom didn't hold back. Her spankings weren't just humiliating, they *hurt*. She had very strong arms and wasn't afraid to put the force of her anger behind them.

Even though my mother warned him, Sam wasn't aware that he would *actually* get a spanking, since his mother didn't spank him. This was unusual for a kid during the '70s, when the running debate wasn't whether or not to spank your kids but rather what method of spanking was most effective—bare hand, wooden spoon, or leather belt?

But Joan had a degree in child development, so instead of telling her kid how to act and then bringing the hammer down when he didn't *act right*, Joan reasoned with him, employing a tone typically reserved for fragile diplomatic negotiations between hostile nations. "Sam, do you feel ready to share again?" Joan would ask, and then she'd wait patiently as Sam distractedly stared at his feet for approximately the same amount of time that it would've taken my mom to whip out her wooden spoon and whack me on the ass with it.

But Joan wasn't there that day. Expecting that his hostile escalations would be greeted with more high-level peace talks, Sam tossed some more sand my way, only to find himself snatched up, laid across my mother's knee, and spanked. My mom says that she took it easy on Sam—it was more of a warning spank than anything else—but I remember the look on his face. *"How could this be happening?!"* his eyes seemed to ask as they filled with tears, his soft and pretty view of the world dissolving before me like a cherry Icee on hot asphalt.

When Joan found out, she was furious. Here she was, drawing up extensive treaties between herself and her sons, discussing policy decisions ad nauseam, taking pains to employ the gentlest tone possible, and my mom ruined all of that patient, studied diplomacy with one moment of ruthless savagery.

My mom wasn't interested in Joan's knowledge of child development. My mom had double-majored in math and psychology at the University of Illinois, and she'd learned just enough about Freud and Erikson and the rest of those arrogant assholes to proclaim it all complete horseshit. Of course she'd also read *I'm OK—You're OK* and Dr. Spock, but that didn't mean she'd lost her head completely. Everyone knew that no matter what the hand-holding experts might say, when kids were very, very bad and they weren't listening, only one thing set them straight, and that was a good, hard smack.

That night Joan called, but my mom didn't apologize. All the kids in her care had to follow the same rules, she explained calmly. Joan burst into tears, shocked that my mom wouldn't back down. "I guess this is the end of our friendship," she told my mother.

That made my mom laugh. "You're not getting rid of me that easily, so don't even think of it," she said. "We're going to be friends for the rest of our lives."

ALTHOUGH THEY LEARNED to tread lightly around matters of discipline, Christine and Joan and my mom continued to experiment with how much they could or should lean on each other. In keeping with this test of interdependence, my mom left us with Joan and her family one night while she went on an out-of-town trip. My brother and sister didn't want to go to Joan's house, but at age nine, I was happy for this rare chance to get a close-up look at how another family functioned. Did they spend most of their time bickering about the rules of Risk or Monopoly, punching each other, and then sulking in their rooms like we did? And if not, how did they fill up their free time?

From the first few minutes alone with Joan's family, we could see they were floating in a completely different galaxy from ours. Joan's house was filled with modern designer furniture, all leather and chrome and glass, with Bauhaus chairs and Flokati rugs and enormous Warhol prints on the walls. Sam and his little brother Felix had big rooms filled with lots of expensive toys we didn't have at home, thousands and thousands of Legos and wooden building blocks that somehow seemed fancy and European to us, even though we hardly knew what that meant.

That night, Joan enlisted our help making chicken à la king. I could tell by the way she peeled the eggs and chopped the chicken, hesitantly, consulting her shiny new cookbook every few minutes, that she didn't cook very often. She probably couldn't bake a cherry pie. There were frozen Pepperidge Farm apple turnovers in the freezer, along with a stack of Stouffer's frozen entrees.

The chicken was a little bland, but we had really good Swiss chocolate for dessert. Then Harry broke out these red cushions on sticks that looked sort of like upholstered baseball bats—more imported toys that we could only conclude were Europe's answer to a child's recurring urge to beat other children about the face and neck. At my house, we would've just improvised with pillows or couch cushions or *actual* baseball bats, if they were handy, but at Joan's that would've constituted "roughhousing," which was strictly forbidden. At Joan's house, you used words, not fists, to make your point—unless there was an imported toy involved, purchased specifically to allow your high-energy, somewhat willful children to express their feelings of frustration and longing in an appropriate manner.

Even so, it only took a few minutes of fun with the upholstered baseball bats before Sam got carried away and knocked Felix off his feet by swiping his bat across Felix's wobbly knees. Felix fell down on the shiny hardwood floor and cried that Sam wasn't playing nice, and then it was time for a family conference. Harry, Joan, Sam, and Felix all gathered to discuss the fact that Sam needed to tone it down a little, and no, the point of the game wasn't to knock Felix off his feet, the point was to have *fun* and to sort of *pretend* to fight, but to do so *gently* and *without malice*.

My brother and sister and I stood there on the sidelines, gawking at the inefficiency of this family's bureaucratic dealings. Why didn't they just smack Sam across his smart-ass face and move on? But then we got bored and climbed the stairs to Sam's room to play with his enormous stockpile of Legos. Sam and Felix joined us a few minutes later, but Sam got mad at Laura for hogging all the roof pieces for her split-level home and then Felix wet his pajamas and finally we crawled into our sleeping bags and stared at the ceiling, thinking about how young and bratty Sam and Felix both were, how their parents were making them soft in the middle, dooming them to get their asses kicked with clocklike regularity for the balance of their days on earth.

But those two boys were still sort of our friends, because our mothers were friends and our fathers worked together. Even when we were jealous of them or wanted to hit them in the face or felt sorry for them, they were still a little bit like cousins. We sort of cared about them in a weird way, and anyway, we had to tolerate them and bite our tongues as much as possible. Kids that whiny and pathetic obviously needed us as friends. If we weren't nice to them, who would be?

The next day, I told my mom how we had made chicken, but it had taken a long time and we didn't eat until late. "Joan doesn't cook that much," she responded, with a tone that suggested that, sure, Joan had an advanced degree, sure, she had expensive furniture and art on the walls of her big house, but Joan still wasn't quite as capable as my mom was.

Joan's parents didn't have a lot of money, she explained, but her mother was obsessed with how rich people lived, constantly comparing their impoverished lives with those of the Vanderbilts or some other wealthy family. Joan's mother used to tell her that she looked fat, and it gave her a complex and now she has trouble with her weight. Joan had been through a lot. Sometimes she struggled just to be happy.

It made me wonder what Joan told her kids about my mom.

THE NEXT SUMMER, when my parents' divorce was almost final, Joan upped the stakes and invited my mom and us kids to stay at a beach house she'd rented. This sounded hopelessly luxurious to me. Typically, my family would drive to Myrtle Beach and stay at our favorite little mom-and-pop hotel, the Shorecrest, for a long weekend, swimming at the beachside pool and building sand castles and going for long walks by the water until we were tired and sunburned and covered in a thin layer of salt and sand. But five days at a rented house? That was the kind of thing that *rich* families did. So we cheerfully packed our clothes and babbled giddily in the car and gasped over the huge, pretty house right on the beach, then went along with whatever sleeping arrangements and table-clearing and dish-washing schedules our moms had dreamed up for us.

Everything was going surprisingly well, in fact, until Felix, age three and a half, inspired perhaps by the sudden proximity of two older girls, decided that he was done with being a boy. He wanted to be a *girl*.

Naturally we all expected Joan to tell Felix in no uncertain terms that he was a boy, like it or not, and there was nothing he or anyone else could do about it. Instead, Joan sat and listened closely to Felix's heartfelt desires. That alone seemed odd to us. How was this an occasion for listening? In our house, at the very most, Felix would've received a brief lecture, one that began with the words "Life isn't fair" and ended with the words "tough shit." But Joan wanted to understand and empathize.

After a long talk, Joan and Felix decided that Felix should be able to *try out* being a girl for a little while. So Joan put Felix's longish hair in two pigtails, and then she asked that we all refer to Felix as "Felicia" for the rest of the week.

The snickering and eye-rolling that followed weren't dampened either by Joan's disappointment in us or by my mother's somewhat halfhearted requests that we try to respect whatever stupid fantasy scenarios Joan and Felix had invented together. Empowered by his mother's indulgence, Felicia himself would scream and cry if we referred to him as Felix or sneered at his ponytails, and that would send Joan into the room, sharply insisting that we not berate Felicia or call *her* unfair names. We needed to think about how *she* felt, and be more sensitive to *her* feelings. Each use of the wrong pronoun made us giggle, which made even more big, salty tears roll down Felicia's face.

In the end, it was Sam who couldn't take it anymore. He was eight years old, just old enough to be horribly embarrassed by his mother's soft spot for the delicate folds of burgeoning gender-identity issues.

"It's so *stupid!*" he yelled at her. "Felix is *not* a girl! *Pigtails* don't make you a girl!"

Instead of shaking her fists at Sam and telling him that *Felix was a girl if she said so, goddamn it,* Joan started addressing Sam's feelings about Felix's feelings about being a girl, and Felix's feelings about Sam's feelings about Felix's feelings, and Joan's feelings about everyone's feelings and on and on and on until my two siblings and I retreated to our rooms to whisper about how dumb it all was, and how could we possibly make it all week with these weirdos?

In our house, the slightest deviation from the behavior deemed acceptable by the majority was quickly and harshly snuffed out by an avalanche of open scorn and ridicule. You didn't dare to discuss anything remotely sensitive around my family, let alone parade around with pigtails in your hair, pretending you were something that you clearly weren't and would never, ever be. What you actually wanted, deep inside, was so far from the point, it could only be treated as a punch line.

We didn't go to the beach with Joan again.

· · ·

EVENTUALLY, all three of the faculty wives divorced their respective jackasses. Christine was the first to get divorced. My mom was next. The summer I turned nine years old, she told my father she wanted a separation, then moved into a studio apartment across town for a few months so my dad could look after us while she spent her time looking for a full-time job. Just when Joan's marriage looked like it might survive the long haul, she started to suspect that her husband was cheating on her.

Christine or my mother would've shrugged it off or quietly filed for divorce. But not Joan. Joan hired a private investigator. And when the private investigator proved himself inept, Joan started sleuthing herself. After a few crafty phone calls and some stealthy driving around town, Joan determined that the other woman was married, and actually had a kid who attended a nearby school. Joan needed to know more about this woman. So she watched her one day, playing with her kid in the yard of the school, running around in circles with her arms outstretched like an airplane.

Joan couldn't believe it. *This* was the woman who would end her marriage? She was likable enough, but was she beautiful? Not really. Was she charming and special? Not as far as Joan could tell. Could she bake a cherry pie? Maybe, who cared? Joan almost felt disappointed, to have been defeated by someone so ordinary, so unimpressive. It seemed that, in this case, *The* Other Woman, was really just *Some* Other Woman.

My mother's song about Billy Boy and his unrealistic culinary requirements always implied that marriages were built and eventually fall apart based on some quantifiable set of qualities or deficits in the husband and wife involved. But Harry hadn't traded up, he had simply *traded*. In the end, it seemed that most marriages were like old teddy bears that you simply outgrew one day. It wasn't personal, even as you set them on fire, then stepped back to watch them burn.

OVER THE YEARS, Joan and Christine and my mom quit smoking. Coffee was replaced by decaf and hot tea. Homemade pie was replaced by the chocolate mousse or fruit tart my mom picked up at the new high-end grocery on Broad Street. But the talking and shouting and cackling were the same. Even as they grew older and worked full-time jobs, after their husbands were long gone, the three of them still met regularly to talk for hours at a time.

They also started to go to the beach together each year. Without kids to deal with, it was much easier to look past their differences and just enjoy each other's company. Sometimes the men they were seeing would come along, and some years they went alone instead, because one of them wasn't seeing anyone or because that year they thought, why bring anyone else? What they really wanted was that time they could spend, just the three of them, shutting out the world around them.

Then Joan was diagnosed with lupus. My mother dealt with it the only way she knew how: she gathered information. She and Christine and Joan had already been touring continuous-care retirement communities—places they might move to together when they were still healthy, that offered varying levels of care as they became older and less able to care for themselves. After Joan got sick, though, they started touring assisted-living facilities. These were essentially nursing homes, far less cheerful than the more expensive continuous-care places. After a few weeks, my mom wanted to know: Joan, what's your plan?

Joan didn't have a plan. Joan wanted my mom to spend the night at her condo. Joan wanted Sam and Felix to come and live with her for a while. Joan was worried about dying in her sleep. Joan didn't want to take her medication, because she didn't like how it made her feel. After years of being a capable woman, a woman who ran her own catering business, a woman who raised two children and endured Felix's tours of duty in Iraq (presumably without pigtails), Joan was falling apart.

She couldn't sleep at night. She didn't want to know any more about those assisted-living places. She wanted someone—an old friend or one of her sons—to take care of her.

The last thing my mom wanted was to take care of anyone, outside of her high-maintenance Jack Russell, Chloe. She was philosophically opposed to it. My mom still felt the same way that she felt thirty years before, when she stood in the kitchen, singing and rolling out the dough for her pie: A woman should always find a way to take care of herself. Of course it's nice to feel valuable and attractive to both men and women, but ultimately a smart woman knew that she was on her own. She had to make a plan, to secure her own survival—or even to map out her eventual demise—independently.

Because you can't always depend on men or your female friends or even your children—not really. They have their own lives, after all. People can't be expected to drop everything and take care of you. Believing that they should will only make you weak and feeble, and who wants to live that way? For my mother, the most terrible fate in the world is wanting something from someone that they can't or won't give you. That's the last thing she'd ever do.

This attitude had lingered in the background of my mother's behavior for years, the way she felt most problems could be solved with lots of hard work, the way she waved off the whole notion of "stress" as if it were merely a side effect of procrastination and laziness. It was inconceivable to my mom that anyone could have a bad feeling that couldn't be cleared up by taking down the storm windows and washing them, or going to the office before sunrise and tackling a bunch of tasks before anyone was there to interrupt you. Analyzing life's heaviest challenges with your friends was one thing, but would you actually call them when you were falling apart? No way.

Even before Joan's diagnosis, my mom had been going through a crisis of her own, thanks to her growing dread over the prospect of retiring from her longtime job as business manager of the neurobiology department at the university. It made her anxious to tour those assisted-living places, filled with old people being wheeled around awful rooms with ugly curtains and flocked wallpaper. Although my mom took in her own mother when she got too old to take care of herself, she couldn't accept the same scenario for herself. Who wants to be planted in the middle of your kid's life, only to drive each other crazy? Most of all, she didn't want to talk about it.

"Look, I'm just retiring," she said to me a few months before she left her job last year, when she found out that her office was planning a party for her, a party that she promptly called off. "I don't want anyone making a big deal about it. Everyone wants to know *what I'm going to do*! I don't *know* what I'm going to do, but I'm not depressed about it! It's not the end . . . it's just the *beginning* of the end, that's all."

"God, that sounds awful," I said.

She scoffed at this. "No it's not, I'm looking forward to it, I am. . . . I just hate to burn through a bunch of money when I get too old to know the difference. Sometimes I think it would be nicer to give it to someone young, who could *really* enjoy it."

"It's your money. Who cares what someone else would do with it?"

"Look, I'm not saying I want to die! I'm just saying it wouldn't be the worst thing in the world if I got some incurable disease . . ."

"Are you kidding?"

"Heather, not *now*! Of course not! I mean, in a while. But when the time comes, I'd like to just take an overdose. I don't want to have to linger on and just waste a lot of money for no reason."

"An *overdose*?"

"Not right now! Jesus. I'm just saying that I want to make sure that I *can* take an overdose if I want to, and no one's going to get *all worked up* about it. When the time comes."

"You think everyone's going to say, 'Sure, no problem. Go for it!'"

"Well. It's my choice."

Conversations about retirement always ended there, with talk of incurable diseases and overdoses. Retirement itself wasn't a problem, but *planning* for retirement also required planning for a lot of different, deeply unacceptable possibilities, like growing frail and sick and playing Bingo with people who didn't know their own names. She knew she had to have a plan, but she didn't *really* want to plan for anything, beyond, say, securing a lethal dose of pills and hiding them somewhere safe.

And now here Joan was, suddenly and unexpectedly providing a front-row glimpse of what dependence and being diagnosed with an incurable disease might actually look like. Of course my mother spent the night with Joan a few times a week and drove Joan to doctors' appointments and did anything else that Joan asked. My mother's loyalty and generosity in the face of crisis were unquestionable. She struggled for months to meet Joan's most irrational demands. But it wore on her, because she would never have asked such things of Joan or Christine or anyone else. And she hated to see this woman, whose assertiveness she'd marveled at over the years, transformed into a timid, needy little mouse.

If my mom were Joan, she might have pointed a gun at her head on the afternoon of her diagnosis. Forget asking a friend to help her to the bathroom in the middle of the night—she'd sooner drive her Honda into a brick wall.

This was the uneasy truth behind my mom's song: My mother wanted to be needed, but she never wanted to need anyone else. *She* would be the one baking cherry pies. *She* would be the one cleaning gutters and painting ceilings and pulling ivy out of the backyard. This is so often the paradox of truly, astoundingly capable people.

They're never quite capable of sitting back and allowing the people around them to be the capable ones.

FOR THE PAST MONTH, whenever I hear my mom talk about Joan's latest struggles with her health, I think: I'm more like Joan. Sure, I'm reasonably responsible. I like to have a plan. But I still cling to some romantic notion of being taken care of. I still imagine that I won't be alone in the end, however unrealistic that might be. Where my mom pictured herself alone, having to fend for herself, even back when she was married—with a philandering husband, she probably felt that she was on her own most of the time—I always pictured myself enlisting someone to go along for the ride with me, no matter what my circumstances might be.

If I get sick or lose my mind, I'll ask my husband or my kids or my friends to rise to the occasion and come to my aid. And they'd better come through for me, goddamn it! I refuse to be the one driving myself down to the pharmacy for my lethal dose of something or other, then swallowing it alone in my bedroom. Instead, I'll be the pest on the phone to my daughters, begging them to fly into town, squandering my money on plane tickets, or planting myself on the couch in the den, much to some son-in-law's chagrin. I'll bring my dog with me, too, and it'll sleep on the couch with me and beg at the dinner table and everyone will roll their eyes at how weird and gross Grandma is.

Can she bake a cherry pie, Billy Boy, Billy Boy? *Once* she could. Now she buys frozen pies at the store, even though we had pie last night and the night before. Grandma doesn't really listen, and she needs help with her disgusting old slippers, and she made us install a geriatric bar and a rubber mat in the bathtub so she can get in and out without breaking her hip, and she laughs really loudly at stuff that's not funny, like TV anchormen and our friend's names and the lyrics to pop music.

At some point before I'm too old, I'll sit my daughters and my husband and my closest friends down, and I'll warn them: *I'm not growing old alone, motherfuckers. Prepare yourselves now to see my nasty old face in your house for years to come.*

Because I did my part. I dried your tears and paid too much for replicas of lost teddy bears on eBay. I took care of cats and plants and talked you through home purchases and career dilemmas and bad breakups and cowrote scathing letters to exes that were never sent, but which served as an important catharsis to a breaking heart. I was there for you. And I'll continue to be there, as long as I can be.

But someday, you might have to come to my rescue. Brace yourselves, because it won't be pretty. Isn't that what love and friendship are really about? You reap the benefits first—the long talks over strong coffee or strong beer—then you pay on the back end, when everyone is falling to pieces.

But we weren't meant to suffer alone! We weren't meant to pay strangers to take care of us, then meet our friends or family for an hour-long lunch. We weren't meant to overdose in our bedrooms, just to escape the indignity and frustration of asking for help, for needing help, from someone who might not always enjoy giving it, someone who gets on our nerves, who has never made much sense to us, someone whom we break down and bicker with occasionally. We were meant to lean on each other, as messy and imperfect as that can be, to be capable when we can, and to allow the world to take care of us when we can't.

It won't be *all* bad. Or it will be. But at least we'll have each other.

4

Jesus Must Die

The day God disappeared into thin air and never came back, we'd arrived five minutes late for the eight-thirty mass at Sacred Heart Catholic Church. Since most of the pews were filled already, my family and I climbed the stairs to the balcony to sit on a lonely bench that looked down on the whole church and the priest, that tiny figure in white-and-gold robes droning on in the distance. It almost felt silly to sit, stand, and kneel up there along with the congregation below, but we went through the motions anyway.

My parents were always reluctant to sit in the middle of the church. Just like at the movie theater, where they'd insist on leading us to seats at the very front or the very back, they refused to place themselves in the midst of a writhing throng of people. The truth was that they'd rather swallow broken glass than insert themselves into the bosom of the community with an open heart.

I was seven years old and I liked sitting up so high above everyone else. Unfortunately, though, there weren't enough distractions in the balcony to keep me busy—no rolls of fat smashed into the starched collar of a pressed white shirt and suit coat a few inches from my face as I knelt, no squirming toddlers whose bad behavior I could feel smugly superior to, no close-up view of the liberal Catholic hippies with their guitars and tambourines and warbling voices singing "Morning Has Broken" for the fourth time that month. There was just the black-and-brown wicker railing that separated our narrow balcony seats from the collective heads and backs of the whole church. Sitting on the hard wooden pew, I would unfocus my eyes until the wicker swam in black and brown swirls as, just beyond that, the obedient faithful mumbled, "We believe in the Father. . . . We believe in one Catholic and apostolic Church. . . . We believe in the forgiveness of sins, the resurrection of the dead, and the life everlasting."

We believe, we believe, we believe. As I made my vision go blurry that day and the bass tones of that almost grouchy-sounding chorus of Catholics rumbled beneath me, I found myself wondering: Why doesn't God or Jesus just show up and *talk* to us, so we don't have to do all of this exhausting *believing*? If the Almighty One and His heavenly cohorts could simply materialize, it sure would save us the time and effort and the countless inconveniences of *hope* and *faith* and *trust* and the like. And shouldn't *God personally thank us* every now and then, for singing His praises each Sunday?

Then it struck me: Maybe everyone in the church that day was wrong! Maybe we all—every one of us—believed in things that *didn't actually exist*. Maybe we insisted on repeating our beliefs over and over and over again *precisely because* it was such a colossal leap of faith to believe any of these things in the first place, when none of us had any real proof.

Suddenly I felt very small. The whole church seemed very small. All of the people in it seemed very small, and confused. Who were we talking to?

WHEN KIDS at my Catholic school wondered about the existence of God, they usually talked about how there was some shroud that proved that Jesus existed, some bloody loincloth in Rome or Bethlehem, that Christ wore on the cross. This was discussed with the same air of speculation that surrounded talk of how Mikey, from the Life cereal commercials, had died from drinking Coke and eating Pop Rocks at the same time. We might not have had all the facts ourselves, but we'd *heard* about it, just like we'd heard about modern-day miracle workers like Mother Teresa and Mary Poppins and Santa and Cap'n Crunch.

But not everyone believed it, even in my Catholic school. Ginger Campbell told us one day that not only didn't Santa exist, but *Jesus* didn't exist, either. Apparently her parents had told her years earlier that Santa was just an amusing invention for tricking naive little kids. Her parents didn't believe in God or Jesus, either—which obviously meant they were crazy and a little bit evil. Maybe they were members of a creepy cult like the one my sister and I had seen on *The Edge of Night* one afternoon.

I had no way of knowing then that most religions weren't anywhere near as creepy as Catholicism, with its kneeling and its endless recitations and its continual signing of the cross. I assumed that all other churches and temples must be at least as dreary and morbid as ours, with its monotone priests and its holy water and its cardboard circular Christ-flesh and its chalice of red wine and its obsession—its grim, unyielding obsession—with Jesus' bloody, painful, hideous death before a smelly mob of smudgy-faced, cursing heathens.

Year after year at school we reenacted Jesus' grueling death march. Some sixth-grader would wear a crown of faux thorns and a toga and haul an enormous cross through the church (inevitably whining that it was too heavy, at which point our religion teacher informed the boy, with great relish, that he should consider himself *lucky* to have such a direct taste of the agony Jesus went through on that fateful day). All the girls wanted to be Mary Magdalene, of course, so they could show up in pretty blue robes and mercifully wipe off Jesus' feet—or maybe it was his mother Mary who did that? What was wrong with Jesus, anyway, that he chose a girlfriend with the same name as his mom?

Of course, Judas called Mary Magdalene Jesus' "whore," which obviously meant that she had lots of boyfriends and went around town bathing filthy feet left and right. I had learned the real, behind-the-scenes story from my copy of *Jesus Christ Superstar* at home, which we pulled out and listened to every Easter, mostly because we liked to sing along with "This Jesus Must Die":

> *What then to do about this Jesus mania?*
> *How do we deal with a carpenter king?*
> *Where do we start with a man who is bigger*
> *Than John was when John did his baptism thing?*

But even *Jesus Christ Superstar* got long and rambling after the miracles and the casting-of-money-lenders-out-of-the-temple part. Once you were deep into the suffering and the nailing and the dying and the "My God, My God, why hast Thou forsaken Me?" part, it really dragged. From Jesus' endless solo in the Garden of Gethsemane onward, that story went from a plucky, slightly mean-spirited celebrity romp ("Hosanna Superstar!") to a grisly cautionary tale about the dangers of extreme overconfidence. Anyone could see, when Pontius Pilate was washing his hands of the whole murdering-Jesus affair but Jesus was still smugly insisting on his own omnipotence, that Mary had inflated her son's self-esteem to a risky degree. The guy was just so cocky, you almost *wanted* to see him take a hard fall . . . sort of like Leif Garrett, but without the feathered hair.

And it was frustrating, in *Jesus Christ Superstar* and in the Bible and in that movie starring Charlton Heston, that all of these nonbelievers could get away with hissing and spitting and saying malicious things, while the loyal, the faithful, the good were simply resigned to their horrible fates, passively trudging along to their own agonizing deaths.

The faithful always made faith look so unpleasant.

And maybe we were all wrong, we of the droning congregation in the church that day. Maybe we were kidding ourselves by calling ourselves the chosen ones. Maybe we were actually small and powerless on the face of the enormous earth, reduced to making random guesses about how human beings were meant to occupy their time, then writing down those guesses and repeating them and insisting that *everyone believe in them*.

And maybe the whole globe wasn't enormous at all, in the big scheme of things! Maybe we all existed, the whole world, on a tiny speck of dust, just like the tiny people in *Horton Hears a Who*, which I'd recently seen on TV. In fact, the whole world could just explode or get crushed at any minute! Maybe our speck of dust would get squashed, and no God or angels would appear to announce that it was about to happen, like they said they would in the Bible! We could all perish in an instant, without warning!

Suddenly I wanted to be sitting down there, with the rest of the congregation, quietly muttering about my belief until it felt true. But my faith was shaken.

I NEEDED a concrete sign from God. He would do that for me, wouldn't He? But maybe He didn't like making a big, showy spectacle of Himself. After all, didn't He say, "Don't make gold-encrusted likenesses of My omnipotent face, because it embarrasses the hell out of Me, plus it's just tacky"? But then, maybe He wouldn't mind *privately* demonstrating His existence, if it meant I would be saved from this alarming state of uncertainty. Didn't I pray every night, or at least once every few nights? Wasn't I a good kid, one who clearly deserved some sort of reassurance? Wasn't I meek and humble, at least when I wasn't expecting God to materialize just to squelch my fears?

So I went home after church that day and climbed the stairs to my room and looked for some way for God to give me a sign. Couldn't He move something in my room, or make my teddy bear talk to me, using His voice? No, that seemed a little too magical and extreme, which clearly wasn't God's style, since He hadn't so much as shown His face for centuries now.

I needed something very easy and *subtle* for God to do, something that wouldn't take all that much energy, and something that wouldn't blow my mind completely and make me crazy for the rest of my life. So I took a piece of toilet paper from the bathroom, about one foot long, and placed it on top of my bed. "Okay, God," I thought, concentrating very hard on reaching Him, "please rip this piece of toilet paper in half, and then I'll know You exist. I promise I won't ask for any more proof, ever, for as long as I live."

I left the room, out of respect for God's privacy. I waited in the hallway, hoping my sister wouldn't come upstairs and ask what I was doing, hoping that God would throw me this one little bone and then I wouldn't have to worry that the world could spin off into the abyss or burst into flames or break into a million little pieces, at least not without ample warning and a chance to confess my sins first, so that I had some hope of ascending into heaven, just in the nick of time.

It's odd, really, that so many people believe that religion will give their kids peace of mind and some sense of structure, considering how much darkness and chaos and horror are wrapped up into it. Would the apocalypse even have occurred to me at age seven, had I not been reminded of the day of reckoning, when God comes to judge the living and the dead, *every single Sunday* since I gained consciousness?

And where did it all lead? Not to peace and calm and a heart filled with love, but to an anxious moment in an olive-green-shag-carpeted hallway, where I sat on the top stair, hoping against hope for the Miracle of the Torn Toilet Paper.

BUT A GOOD KID like me *deserved* a miracle. If someone like Dawn Hunt asked God to give her a sign, that would be different.

Of course I knew that God supposedly loved the poor and the downtrodden and those who had turned away from his true and righteous path, like the Prodigal Son. But Dawn Hunt was a million times worse than the Prodigal Son . . .

Which is why, that day in the second grade when I walked into the girl's bathroom and saw shit smeared on the walls and the words "Fuck You" scrawled all over the stalls and the mirrors and the ceiling in red Magic Marker, I didn't think, "Who could've done such a crazy thing?" I thought, "Wow, Dawn Hunt has really outdone herself this time." Among the dutiful Catholics at my school who suspected that God would punish them for merely talking in class, Dawn Hunt stood out like a hungry pit bull at a free-range chicken ranch.

Of course, anonymity is never the troublemaker's goal. Whether she was leaning over the table to write bad words on someone else's worksheet or rolling her eyes and smiling slightly when a teacher yelled at her for the fifty-millionth time, Dawn put her signature touch on every mischievous thing that she did. She took real *pride* in being the very worst kid in our whole class.

As the other best friend of my best friend, Kimberly Shaw, Dawn had a particular interest in tormenting me. She relished getting under my skin. She wasn't a bully. I wouldn't even say that she was mean. She just enjoyed making me extremely uncomfortable.

"Psst. Psst. Heather." This was Dawn, sitting behind me in social studies. "My poothy hurtth!" she whispered with a twisted smile, affecting a strange lisp for good measure. I hadn't even heard the word "pussy" before Dawn said it. Until she grabbed her crotch, I thought she might be talking about her cat.

I tried not to react. I knew that Dawn was unflappable. Even when the teachers at my school screamed in her face, Dawn would just sit there, her eyes half closed, smiling like some skinny, disheveled, redneck Mona Lisa.

But you had to give it up for Dawn, at some level. The girl had real flair. She wore smudgy black eyeliner in the second grade. She knew how to flip her hair just like Kristy McNichol before anyone else did. She pranced around in skintight jeans and T-shirts with glitter on them that said things like "Foxy Lady!" The girl walked into the front doors of Sacred Heart Catholic School every morning looking like a truck-stop whore, and everyone, even the most fearsome nuns, seemed flummoxed over what to do about it.

Every afternoon, the bus dropped Dawn off in front of a dreary brick apartment building. I never saw her parents. She always seemed to be moving through the world alone.

Of course, this is part of the irony of Catholic school: You get the most obedient, rule-following, God-fearing children, members of huge families with parents whose only resort for dealing with behavior problems is a quick and brutal spanking before returning to their assembly line of peanut-butter-and-jelly sandwiches in the kitchen. Then you throw these timid team players in with a handful of the most hardened cases in the whole town. There was only one Catholic school in Durham, so there was only one hard-assed, intolerant, scary-strict place for the parents of really bad kids to turn to when their kids were kicked out of every other public and private school in sight.

In fact, every single class in my elementary school had one horrifically bad kid. In my sister's grade, it was Ken Buttrell, an aggressive bully who'd punched and kicked and bitten several kids. I saw Ken jump onto my brother's back out of nowhere like a hungry mountain lion leaping onto an oblivious, peace-loving antelope. That kid made me hold my breath every time I ran into him. But if the Catholics kicked him out, where would he go? The teachers seemed to recognize that these kids were irredeemable, even as they ripped their hair out trying to tame them.

The rest of us knew that we should feel lucky that we were different from Dawn and Ken and the other bad kids at my school. We should feel lucky that our parents loved us enough to hit us with leather belts and wooden spoons when we were bad.

But if there really was no God, then why *not* be bad? What was the point of being good? Maybe Billy Joel was right, when he sang that song about how the sinners have much more fun— the one that my father wouldn't let us listen to.

EVEN IF THE SINNERS had nothing but fun, I still longed for the reassurance of an all-powerful God to look after me. Because the safest and most uneventful childhood still held a gauntlet of unspeakable horrors: enormous cockroaches that wriggle their way into the bathroom and crawl out at your most vulnerable moment, neighborhood dogs that get hit by speeding cars right in front of your eyes, knees that bust open on the pavement and afford a disconcerting glimpse of muscle and bone, gerbils that run out of fresh water and are later discovered, two of them eating the third one alive.

Sure, my mom tried to make us feel better about the scary things in the world. But somehow she always managed to let her own nihilistic views filter in through the cracks in what she said. When our family cat disappeared and my dad found him dead in the backyard, I asked my mom where cats go when they die. "Well . . ." she began, hesitantly, "*some* people believe that cats— and people—go to heaven, where they're much happier than they were here on earth."

"What do *you* believe?" I asked, but her subsequent rambling suggested that she wasn't quite willing to lay out the full gloomy nature of her views on the subject. I got the idea, though. She didn't believe in anything at all.

I figured my mom was just weird. Weirdos and nonbelievers and heretics were in the Bible, after all. But they were clearly a very quiet minority, an aberration.

I didn't put together a darker possibility until that day in church, and then afterward, tiptoeing back into my room, so as not to disturb God, only to find the toilet paper in one piece, in the exact same place where I left it. Reciting beliefs over and over was a hopeless cause. It would never change the fact that the world was a frightening place, filled with wild, unruly, bad people. Kids like Ken Buttrell and Dawn Hunt could curse and smear crap on the walls and bite people and complain that their poothies hurt and it didn't matter. Lightning would never strike them down.

My good behavior would never pay off the way everyone promised it would. The toilet paper was unmoved. The heavens refused to send me relief. I wasn't safe from a cold, uncaring, unpredictable universe. Either God didn't exist, or He was too busy or detached to bother. Either way, it didn't bode well for me.

5

D-I-V-O-R-C-E

One day his mother said,
When Pierre climbed out of bed,
"Good morning, darling boy!
You are my only joy."
Pierre said, "I don't care."

My mother is hiding. We can see her through the window, looking for a place in the tiny studio apartment where she can't be seen. Finally, she opens a door, we glimpse a flash of toilet and shower and white tile, and she ducks in and closes the door behind her.

"Don't you want to see your kids?" my father is bellowing in the window at her. "What's wrong with you?" Now he's circling the side of the apartment building, through the grass, around the hedge, to a small window outside the bathroom. He raps on the window. "Don't you want to see your children?"

Doesn't she want to see her children? We've stopped by

unannounced, I know that. This is another one of my dad's Very
Bad Ideas, one that's calculated to piss off my mom. I know that
it's not fair of him, to drive by the apartment my mom is renting
for the summer, to spot her rental car outside and realize that we
have her trapped. Of course he walks right up and rings the
doorbell, and when she doesn't answer, even as we urge him to
get back in the car, he has to look in the windows anyway.

He's obviously looking for a fight. What else can she do but
hide? Is she supposed to just stand there, in the strange little space
she's subletting, with its sleeper sofa and its upside-down ten-
speed bicycle hanging from the ceiling and its enormous poster
of a very speedy-looking yellow motorcycle on the wall? Is she
supposed to sit there, on the edge of the sofa, and let us peer in
the windows at her like she's an animal at the zoo?

No. But we can't stop looking, either. This is our first glimpse
of where she's been living for the past two weeks, and we're curious, but also horrified. What does she do all day, without us?
Why would she want this? It's impossible to think of her sleeping on
that pull-out sofa under that yellow motorcycle every night. She
always told us that motorcycles weren't safe. On a motorcycle,
there's no protection around you. You might as well be hurtling
through the air. What good will a helmet do, when you're rocketing around like a missile? You can still break your back or your
neck. Your bike can fall sideways on the street and you can get
run over by another car. You might even get someone else killed
while you're at it. Motorcycles are for reckless idiots who don't
care about anyone but themselves.

A reckless idiot must live in this apartment. The place feels as
out-of-character for my mom as the whole choice to move out,

to get some time and some space to herself, *to think*. Who needs time *to think*? Who needs *space* away from her own family? My mother, who's always home, for better or for worse.

My mother, always home. When I was very small, I had her to myself. My dad went to work and my brother and sister went to school and the house grew quiet. When they left, my mother softened, time slowed down, lunchtime came and went, the sunny afternoon stretched out before us: sitting on a blanket spread out in the backyard with me by her side in the springtime, birds chirping above us, the smell of pine straw, the echoes of a lawn mower next door, the Germans cutting their perfect grass again. My mother hummed to herself as we gazed up at the tall pine trees, swaying several stories above us, a moving canopy casting shadows and speckles of sunlight across the blanket. When I had my mom to myself, she spoke in melodious, enthusiastic tones. She listened. She pointed to birds and squirrels. She told stories. She sang.

There was no press of time, no schedule, no one to interrupt us. We could take in the sunshine, smell the air. We were one and the same, calm and happy, a perfectly matched pair, melting into the spring day, drifting with the clouds, swaying with the tall pines. We feel a chill as a cloud passes in front of the sun; then the warmth and light return and we relax again. There's prickly pine straw beneath the blanket, under my hand. An ant meanders across a stretch of blanket, my mother brushes it away. The sun, the sky, the tall trees, my mother. Always home.

But now she's hiding in a tiny bathroom, as my father raps on the window. Even though I know he's not playing fair—he never is—I also wonder, *Doesn't she want to see her own kids?*

I've never seen her this way, as someone who could freely walk away from me, as someone who would *want* to walk away. Here we are, her kids, and she's in there, standing in the shower in her shoes, waiting for us to leave.

As we get back in the car, my father grumbling about how selfish and crazy my mom is, I wonder how long it'll take for her to come out of the bathroom. When she finally does, she'll breathe a sigh of relief. Alone again, just like she wanted. Then she can relax and enjoy her new, dangerous life, away from us. When we leave, she'll have some *space* again, and some time to *think*.

So much thinking seems dangerous to me. Thinking, all alone, in a tiny apartment? There's no protection around you. You might as well be hurtling through the air. What good will your children do, when your thoughts are rocketing around like missiles? Thoughts like that can break your family into pieces. Thinking is for reckless idiots who don't care about anyone but themselves.

LAURA AND I spent that summer at the neighbor's house across the street. The oldest boy and girl were just a few years younger than we were, but they respected our authority, taking orders and assuming whatever roles we assigned to them in the productions of *Star Wars* and *Dynasty* and *The Love Boat* we created on our tape recorder, complete with commercial breaks. We would lie on the wall-to-wall carpeting of their living room, our faces in the microphone, singing

Bum, Bum, Bumble Bee, Bumble Bee tuna!
I love Bumble Bee, Bumble Bee tuna!

There was something sad about that one. Only someone who was unbearably lonely and pathetic would sing about their love for canned tuna fish. But you never knew how unhappy anyone really was, did you? I was starting to see how adults often put a brave face on things, when really, deep inside, they were falling apart. My parents hadn't been happy *for a long time*, that's what my mom said before she left. She and my dad had called us into their room when we got back from camp. Just sitting in that room, something heavy in the air, our parents' eyes avoiding ours, made me nervous.

"I'm moving out for the summer," my mom began, "because Daddy and I need some time away from each other."

"What?" She might as well have said that she was really a robot or an alien from another planet. *Moving out?* How was that even possible? It was pure insanity to imagine her walking out the front door with a suitcase. Why in the world would she do *that*?

"This isn't your fault. It's important for you to know that."

"What do you mean you're moving out?!"

"I need to, because I'm not happy. *We're* not happy. *But it has nothing to do with you.*"

"Yes *you are* happy! You're fine!"

"No, I—we haven't been happy for a long time."

"Speak for yourself!" my father interjected.

"But that doesn't mean you have to go live somewhere else! You just have to be happier here!"

"You'll understand when you're older."

That was the response that killed me, the one my mom turned to in the months ahead, anytime she couldn't come up with anything better to say. But I couldn't imagine what would change when I was older, how any of this would suddenly seem logical. My mother, packing up and moving out, claiming she was unhappy? She might as well have said, "I'm going to cut off all of your hands with this big blade, now, kids. Yes, it's going to hurt, but *it has nothing to do with you! You'll understand when you're older!*"

"Are you getting a divorce?" my sister asked.

"No, this is just a separation. We're just separating for the summer, to see how it goes. As an experiment."

So that became my mantra for the summer: This is not a divorce. *This is just a separation.* Things will go back to the way they were. Until they do, though, I'll be across the street, where things are still the same. At home, my father wakes up late and cooks us fried liver and eggs for breakfast. He calls it "scrapple" and it's disgusting, but we eat it to keep the peace, to show our gratitude for his attempts at being a good parent in my mother's absence. Would it always be this way? No, *this is just a separation.* My father mows the lawn in his running shorts and tube socks, with a dark blue sweatband around the middle of his head. He is determined to keep everything under control, but he takes long naps in the afternoon. Is he depressed? *Things will go back to the way they were.*

We eat chili and hamburgers with homemade fries for dinner a lot, because these are my father's specialties. We try valiantly to act cheerful. But someone is missing. We pass each other in the hall and flinch, not wanting to acknowledge that the center is gone, something is wrong. *This is just an experiment.* If they get divorced, will my mom come back? Will my dad have to leave? Where will he go? How much older will I have to be to understand? I picture myself at twenty-five, saying: *Yes, now I get it!* What mystery will be solved the moment I get older? What discovery will I make that will explain everything? I don't want to wait that long.

Next door, the German is cutting his perfect grass again. It seems like he's out there every day, mowing the lawn or clipping the long, prickly procession of roses that line his front walk. Every now and then I see him emptying Japanese beetle traps, bags full of the shiny green bugs that have accumulated over the weeks, piling on top of one another, wriggling, waiting for someone to save them. Even as they writhe together in a big pile, they hold out hope that someone will come and explain everything—*No hard feelings!*—and set them free.

ONE AFTERNOON as we're lying around the neighbors' dining room, practicing a "Coke adds life" jingle, the doorbell rings. Mrs. Anderson welcomes in a tall black man in a gray suit. The man lugs an enormous vacuum cleaner in the door with him and stands there, greeting us energetically, dwarfing us in the little room, filling every available inch with his booming voice. After introducing his deluxe, multifeatured Kirby vacuuming unit in a tone that suggests it's his closest personal friend, he sets about shining one of Mrs. Anderson's old metal vases, to show off his good buddy's many functions. We forget our taping session and gather around to coo appreciatively as he makes the vase look shiny and new again. Next, he steam-cleans the wall-to-wall carpeting in two rooms, the brown water showing us all the dirt that was hidden, deep in the carpet, dirt that *no one even knew was there*. Then he dusts drapes using a special drape attachment, and the dust gathers on a filter that spells out the word "Kirby." Incredible!

This goes on for well over an hour, with all of us kids marveling at how much better life is about to be with this amazing machine. The Andersons' house is a pigsty. The den smells like a dead rat. When you open the cupboards in the kitchen, roaches scatter. If anyone needs a multipurpose, high-end vacuum cleaner, it's them.

But after what looks like a tense conversation with Mrs. Anderson in the kitchen, the once-cheery man walks over to say good-bye to us, sounding far less upbeat than he did when he came in. When he drags his machine out the front door, it makes knocking, rattling sounds and seems heavier than before.

Confused, I ask Mrs. Anderson why she didn't buy a vacuum cleaner. The carpeting has never looked so good, doesn't she agree? Isn't she impressed? "Are you kidding?! I wasn't going to buy one of those!" she chuckles. "Those things are way too expensive! I just wanted my carpet cleaned."

I look at her, stunned. She has this delighted, incredulous expression on her face, like she's just *so tickled*, to think that I actually believed, all that time, that she was about to buy a Kirby vacuum cleaner! *You mean you actually thought I wanted to buy that thing,* her face says, and suddenly I want to kick her in the teeth. Why do grown-ups always take such pleasure in the things that kids don't understand?

"Did he know all along that you weren't going to buy one?" I ask.

"Well, no!" she answers. "But if he *had* known, my carpet would still be dirty."

"Don't you think that's a little . . . unfair?"

"Oh, he was just doing his job. *That's what he does.*"

We go to the window to watch the salesman load the unwieldy machine into the trunk of his car in the summer afternoon heat. I scan his face for some sign that he's taking this three-hour detour in stride, some hint that he knew the whole thing was a charade, that it's just part of his job, that it's no big deal. His suit is too small for him and pulls at his rib cage as he slams the trunk closed. I can't tell what he's thinking, whether he's annoyed or angry or disappointed or not. He grimaces and wipes the sweat from his brow, then climbs into the front seat of the car and pulls away. He has to be pissed off, doesn't he? Half a day's work, showing people dirt they didn't know was there, all for nothing?

But everything feels a little dark and ambiguous and unresolved that summer. *The Empire Strikes Back* ends with Han Solo in carbon freeze, and we have to wait another four years to see if he ever makes it out and professes his love to Princess Leia. It looks like they'll be together eventually, but we really can't be sure of anything.

Where's your mama gone, little baby blue?

My mom sang this as we waited in the grass outside the church with the red door. My sister was in there, in preschool. On warm days my mom and I would sit together, waiting for Laura to come out of the door.

When my mom sang that song, I pictured a baby in his crib, staring out the window as his mother drove away.

THE WEEKEND after our unannounced visit to my mom's new apartment, our dad drops us off there again, only this time it's all been prearranged. The apartment looks even smaller and stranger from the inside than it did through the windows: a few books about rock climbing and some outdoor-sports magazines litter the coffee table, not the Doris Lessing and John Updike novels that crowd the shelves in our living room at home. The bathroom has one bottle of shampoo, plus some razors left behind by the previous tenant.

"Whose place is this?" I ask my mom.

It belongs to Harry's brother, Joan's brother-in-law. He's out of the country for the summer. Suddenly I want to know everything about him. "Where did he go? Is that his bike? Does he have a motorcycle?"

"I don't know. Maybe." My mom shrugs. She doesn't know him that well. That seems crazy to me. How could you live in someone's apartment and not know anything about him? Why would he want a strange woman renting his space, sleeping on his couch?

The concept of subletting is lost on me, as is the notion that the guy might need the rent money to afford his summer trip. The place just looks cramped and lonely and depressing. It doesn't make any sense.

She tries to cheer us up by mentioning that there's a pond across the street, she's seen fish in it. Maybe we could all go fishing? She pulls two small fishing poles out of a closet stuffed full of winter coats. The three of us shrug noncommittally, still taking in the apartment. We pull books off shelves. We wander into the kitchen, then crowd around the open door of her refrigerator like it's a display at a museum. It's bare, except for a stick of butter, a package of sliced ham, two onions, and a few cans of A&W root beer. We never have those at home.

"Can I have one?"

"Sure." We all take a root beer, then grab the fishing poles and walk out into the swampy summer air, over the scorching-hot parking lot, across the two-lane road to a small pond strangely situated next to an office building and a retirement home. There's greenish algae growing along the sides of the pond, but a small pier sticks out over the murky water. From it, we can see round gray fish darting here and there, where the sunlight hits the water and turns it yellowish green.

Eric stabs a wriggling worm with one of the hooks and drops it into the spot of sunlight. We watch for a few minutes as the fish investigate the worm, then one strikes. When Eric pulls the fish out of the water, it looks smaller and thinner than it did from the pier, with a pale orange streak across its middle.

An hour later, as our cooler grows crowded with the little fish, a frail, white-haired woman walks out to the pier, steadying herself on the arm of a nurse. The nurse says hello to us, but the woman just stares, then reaches into her pocket and fumbles with a plastic bag for several minutes. Out comes a slice of white bread. "Here, fishies, fishies, fishies!" the old woman calls in a wavering voice. "Lunchtime! That's right, I have your lunch for you!" A gnarled hand rips pieces off the slice of bread and shakily tosses them into the water. "Heeeere, fishies!" She's on the other side of the pier from us, still just a few feet from where our lines dip into the water.

Here, fishies. Take your pick: bread or worms. Will you feast on a free lunch, or will you be *our* free lunch?

We look at each other and, without saying anything, quickly gather up our stuff, whisper good-bye softly, and scramble back over the gravel path to the apartments across the street. Even my mom seems a little chastened.

"That was weird," I offer as we reached her front door.

"Yeah. I felt a little guilty. I've never seen her before. She obviously goes out there every day and feeds them."

I slump onto the sleeper sofa, and stare at the wall, feeling defeated. For a minute there, before the old woman came, things almost seemed normal. We joked around and sang "A&W root beer's got that frosty-mug taste!" and made the fake mug-hands around our cans of root beer the way they did in the commercials. Our mom was still our mom, we could see that. We could still do fun things together. Maybe she hadn't really changed. Maybe she wasn't lost and gone forever. She did say, again, that it was temporary, that it was just for the summer.

Once the old lady came out and called to her fish friends, though, everything went dark again. Our attempts at making this strange visit seem cheerful felt a little desperate, like those jingles we sang, so bright and peppy, always trying so hard to make things like tuna fish and root beer seem exciting and hopeful. But how could we be hopeful, considering the enormous unknowns at play here, the countless things we wouldn't understand until we were older? Those things were obviously so frightening and ugly that they couldn't possibly be explained now. Seeing my mom's life away from us didn't make it any more acceptable. It was fundamentally *unthinkable* for her to live somewhere else. The sun had burned out, the sky was falling.

But we're not happy. It added up, of course. The enraged shouting, the flying sandwiches, the goddamned sorry sons of bitches, the standoffs. But these were all part of the woodwork of our lives together, as a family. What mattered most was that *no one was going anywhere.* Hellish though it sometimes was, it was *our* hell. Our parents fought, we fought with our parents, we fought with one another. Isn't that just how families are?

But if it all led to our family falling apart, then that redefined our entire lives as tragic. And what if our mom left for good? What if plenty of space and time to think made her realize how great it would be to stay away from us forever? How could I even keep living, without her?

Where's your mama gone? She was by your side, every minute of every day, and then one day she was gone. *This is only temporary,* she said. But you wake up in a half-empty house, your father is out running, your mother is across town, over the railroad tracks, sitting alone in her kitchen, drinking coffee and thinking, thinking. She was yours, and she's gone. She was the one person who loved you the most, but that was when you were little, and more lovable. You're bigger and harder to love now, with sharp elbows and dumb questions. *When will you come back?*

Had she wanted to leave since that day in Kansas, when she sat down at a picnic table and refused to get up? Is this the dirt we couldn't see all those years? Was anything in our lives purely good, through and through? Was anyone purely generous? Bread or worms, a free lunch or a feast with strings attached. I was a baby and she loved me, but maybe she needed me then and she doesn't need me anymore. I'm big now, and she's gone. When will she come back?

At the end of the summer, she says, but I don't believe her, as she stands cleaning the biggest of those very small fish, frying them with butter and onions for lunch. They're tasty, but it's hard to avoid their little bones, and we're still hungry afterward.

ONE NIGHT IN LATE AUGUST, my father makes us chili for dinner. We each sit down with a bowl in front of us, ready to eat, and he tells us that my mom is moving back home and he's moving out. They're getting divorced.

There's the word we've feared, the word that my parents have struggled not to use until now. *Not* temporary, *not* just a separation. Divorce. Permanent. We will be three kids and a mother, three kids and a father, but not a whole family anymore. My father doesn't want the divorce, he says. He'll be forced to move out, though, to live alone in an apartment somewhere.

He'll be *lonely*! I stare down at my chili and tears well up in my eyes, warping the chili into a blur of brown and green. Our family is ruined. Divorce! My mom will be back, but *nothing will be the same again.* My mom has a job now. My dad will live alone. Divorce! The world spins around me at a million miles an hour, just a blur of chili to keep me from flying off into some black abyss. There's dirt in the carpet you can't see until you suck it out. The chair, the vase, the drapes—everything is secretly filthy. Everyone puts on a brave face, pretends the world is clean and ordered, pretends they're happy, pretends they're just doing their jobs, pretends that things can stay the same, that no one will leave without warning.

WE THINK THAT our mothers belong to us, that they're made of love and sweetness and kisses and long, sunny afternoons in the backyard. Our mothers—their smell, their smiles, their kind eyes—are part of us. Without them, we might simply disappear.

Of course we all have to get over it—grow up and move on and move out. But my mother's abrupt, premature departure didn't widen my perspective, it darkened it. Even once she came back, nothing was the same. Somehow, if she could just pack her bags one morning and leave, then nothing that I'd ever known could be trusted.

I asked my mother a few months later if she thought Daddy ever cheated on her. She laughed out loud. What a question! Here was that delighted, incredulous look again. *You mean you actually thought your father was faithful? Haven't you been paying attention at all? My God, you don't understand a thing, do you?*

But I had already learned that lesson, the lesson that I didn't understand a thing. And when nothing can be trusted, when one day the world has structure and order and then the next day it makes no sense at all? There's nothing to do but divest. The love you thought surrounded you could be withdrawn at any second. Maybe it wasn't there to begin with. Maybe it's not as strong as you thought, or at least not as important.

She is not everything, your mother. She's just a person. But while my mom and I could talk about anything, intellectualizing the wrinkles in any experience, picking apart the highs and lows, I was never sure about how much I mattered to her. I was fundamentally uncertain. Instead of worrying about it, I decided that it would only be wise to care a lot less.

This was something my parents were good at, after all: You don't need anything from anyone. You just need a little time and space, to think. *Go to your room and think about it,* my mom would say. *Why don't you go to your room? Just spend some time alone, you'll feel better.* The answer wasn't in connection. Salvation could be found in solitude. And so, we withdrew to our rooms, each of us, and we stayed there.

His father said,
"Get off your head,
or I will march you straight to bed!"
Pierre said, "I don't care."

My parents needed to split up. It didn't take that long for me to look at it as a good decision. But something bigger changed the day my mother moved out. She claimed her right to herself, and she refused to apologize for it, or to explain it. This is what happens to a woman who's given too much of herself away. I do understand that, now that I'm older, just like she said I would.

But on some level, her very temporary absence became permanent, because she couldn't claim her own life and still be as close to me. Suddenly I lost her, the mother who spoke in melodious, enthusiastic tones, the one who listened and pointed to birds and squirrels and told stories and sang. She was gone, replaced with lots of time and space, to *think*.

My mother took a full-time job and my father moved out and occupied himself with friends and girlfriends and trips overseas, and the rest of us were left to our own devices, left to our confusion and our indifference. We weren't pressured to spend time together. No one threatened to march us straight to bed. We weren't a family anymore, not really. Just four very different people, and another one, across town. Our mother was back, but we knew now that she didn't belong to us. No one did.

6

Sting Like a Bee

"Float like a butterfly, sting like a bee. See? See? Keep moving, always dancing." My father is bobbing and weaving around the imaginary boxing ring of our back patio, showing off a mean left jab, keeping his gloves up to protect his face while repeating the same words, over and over again.

"Float like a butterfly, and then—bap, bap! Sting like a bee! Too fast, too fast!"

My dad loved Muhammad Ali. He felt that Ali was the perfect antidote to what he saw as the growing wimpiness of his children. We were too shy. We cowered in the face of open conflict or provocation. How did *his* children turn out this way?

Eric was the worst, as far as my dad was concerned. He was the oldest and a boy, but showed little propensity for wrestling or roughhousing or tangling it up in the usual boyish ways. Instead, he drew detailed pictures of airplanes and dragons, or fussily rearranged the little buildings and trees on the elaborate train set in his room. To my father, Eric was far too reserved and soft-spoken. He'd never be able to defend himself against the pushy kids and bullies that reigned in the callous world outside.

My dad didn't notice, but Eric had actually developed a surprisingly adaptive method of avoiding conflict: he'd smirk, shrug nonchalantly, and then quietly slink off when no one was looking. He had honed this approach from dealing with my dad, of course, and employed it whenever my dad started to hold forth on how wimpy he was.

It wasn't a bad strategy, either in our house or in the callous world outside. But my dad was a romantic. He wanted us to use our fists, not words, to solve conflicts. So he brought home two pairs of red boxing gloves one day: an enormous pair for himself, and a slightly smaller pair for Eric that still managed to dwarf his head and upper body, making him look cartoonishly small and frail by comparison.

My brother recognized the importance of appeasing my dad in order to keep the peace. So the two of them retreated to the back patio to bob and weave and jab, my father shouting instructions at him in between blows to the head and body.

For about a year, Eric and my dad boxed regularly. My dad was obviously pretty thrilled at the chance to coach his son into a less faggy existence. But if you watched closely, you'd also notice a faintly malevolent smile lingering on his face, one that told you it was more than a little satisfying to bat the ungrateful son of a bitch around for a while. And even though the whole aggressive exercise went against every cell of my brother's being, his face would darken to a look of angry determination. He was going to get one good shot in somewhere, and my dad was going to *feel* it.

It was oddly relaxing, watching those two, like watching Howard Cosell provoke Ali before a big fight. When Cosell started teasing and prodding, Ali lit up and started talking smack, dancing between menacing threats to his opponent and random philosophical asides.

After Eric had shuffled around, throwing angry punches in the air for a solid half-hour, he'd finally plead exhaustion loudly and vehemently enough that my dad would give him a break. Eric would lie down on the patio in a sweaty heap, and it would be my turn to fight Laura. But if Laura refused to play along with my dad's madness, which was usually the case, then I had to box Eric.

I would put on his absurdly huge gloves and he would begrudgingly put on my father's gigantic gloves. At the sound of the bell—my father's singing *DING DING!*—it was my chance to bounce in my brother's direction, looking for a good opening to land a hard punch.

Instead, I liked to linger in my corner, showing off my butterfly float, jabbing the air. "That's right, Heath. Keep it up. Sting like a bee," my dad would say. "Now *get in there.*"

By this point, Eric was usually standing completely still, his hands by his sides, exhausted and annoyed. "Look at him, he's tired. He's a still target!" my dad would tell me excitedly. "You've got him *just where you want him! Get in there and land a punch!*"

So I'd lower my head and dance over to Eric erratically, hoping that my zigging and zagging would throw him off. I'd duck in and land a gingerly jab on his upper arm—at which point he would put one casual boxing glove on my shoulder and shove me backward several feet across the patio.

"*DING DING!*" my dad would yell, and then, "*Boxers, to your corners!*"

This was my dad's favorite part, the part where he would get up in my face and tell me that the first round had gone really well, I was showing *a lot of heart out there*, but I needed to keep my dukes up and protect my face and body a little better. He'd massage my nonexistent back muscles lightly, as if he were loosening me up, and he'd tell me that I needed to hold my ground better, presumably to make up for the four years and forty pounds between my brother and me, presumably to compensate for my spindly arms that did little more than move food to my mouth and make my Barbie dolls walk around all day and complain to each other in the ugly, whiny voices my sister and I always gave our dolls because for some reason we enjoyed imagining them as highly disagreeable people. Finally my dad would make a big show of toweling off my dry face with the sweaty, smelly hand towel around his neck, and then—"*DING DING!*"—round two began.

I usually lasted about four rounds before I started crying snottily into my hands. But for those four rounds, my dad would act impressed over my fancy footwork, and even though those powerful shoves only reaffirmed what I already knew—that I could be overpowered by almost anyone, including a skinny ten-year-old wimp, and there was nothing I could do about it—I still basked in my dad's attention.

I didn't care that he'd always be holding back a little chuckle that told me it was pretty amusing to watch a six-year-old box her older brother. My dad enjoyed seeing us struggle or squirm or reel in embarrassment, and he wasn't one to hide it.

But I considered myself in on the joke. And no matter how

frustrating or absurd the whole exercise became, each time I put on those gloves, I had a little hope. Ali was the underdog in plenty of matches, wasn't he? He used his wits and his strength and he never stopped moving, never stopped dancing.

ONE NIGHT TWENTY YEARS LATER, my dad died of a heart attack, at the age of fifty-six. I flew home to Durham from San Francisco and, in a terrible, grief-stricken haze, found myself sorting through his things one afternoon, looking for some evidence of something, I don't know what. Mostly I found the heartbreaking traces of a life that ended abruptly: a stained coffee cup in the sink, *Slow Waltz in Cedar Bend* opened by the bed, confused messages on his answering machine.

But in his home office, I found a huge pile of to-do lists written on big yellow legal pads. For the next few hours I couldn't stop reading those lists, searching for clues about this person whom I'd never get to know any better, who'd vanished without fanfare when I'd always expected that we'd have time to understand and respect each other as adults, to bring out the best in each other the way Cosell and Ali did.

I read each word slowly: "Edit manuscripts. Lunch: Papaya. Swim. Make calls. Invoice Kamansky. Diane, 6 p.m., Satisfaction's." This was all that was left. Mundane artifacts of a life, like some illegible scrawlings on the side of a cave that detail trivialities such as the day's weather and the scarcity of big game animals in the area. But just as cave paintings are pondered by hundreds of generations to follow, I squinted at those lists like a tireless archaeologist, until my eyes crossed.

Finally, I came to something that felt significant: a page with notes jotted down during a phone call to a psychic. This was a recent whim of my dad's, after visits to the Unitarian church and passages of Gary Zukav and Rolfing appointments faded in their appeal. First it said: *1994: A productive year. Career is in high gear. Focus on mending relationships.* After that, under 1995, the current year: *Focus on health.* And then, underlined three times: *Keep moving. DON'T GET STUCK.*

BUT PERPETUAL MOTION has its costs. On our cross-country trips together in the years before my parents divorced, my father never made reservations at a single motel. He liked to drive for as long as he could, then wander into some town at sunset, looking for dirt-cheap places to spend the night. While my mother was exhausted and irritated and we kids were hungry and needed to use the bathroom, my dad was energized by the unknowns, even when confronted with "No Vacancy" signs or bad weather.

My dad made choices that invited hassles and stress into his life. He wanted to come close to running out of gas and then *just* make it to the next Stuckey's. He wanted to find the perfect local restaurant on some small road off the beaten path, one that served homemade enchiladas and inspired him to sing "Out in the West Texas town of El Paso, / I fell in love with a Mexican girl!" as we drove off. He wanted to haggle with the silver merchant in Juarez, until the man called out, "See you later, Mr. Jew!" as he walked away.

After cheating on my mom through most of their fifteen-year marriage, my dad started dating several women at once as soon as he got divorced. Occasionally he would refer to one of them as his girlfriend, but he always seemed to have lots of "friends" around, too, young women who'd sit by the pool at his apartment, flipping through magazines or telling us about their days on the pageant circuit. Eventually, there was something in the way he mentioned "Big Nancy" and "Little Nancy" and "Lawyer Nancy" that told us he was sleeping with a few different Nancys at the same time, and that they probably didn't know about each other.

When I pressed him on the matter, he told me that Big Nancy and Little Nancy met once, but Lawyer Nancy didn't know about either of them. But Lawyer Nancy was sort of bossy anyway; she was starting to make demands the second he walked in the door, so she was on the outs. Plus, there was this new woman he'd met at Four Corners the other night. "She has a really incredible figure. I mean, I'm telling you, she looks like Wonder Woman." My dad didn't talk this way with Laura or Eric. He knew Eric would just snort and roll his eyes, and Laura would tell him he was gross and he should go out with women his own age for a change.

But I played the frat boy sidekick. "Wonder Woman? Does she have shiny black hair, too?"

"Brown. But her body is *fantastic*."

I never understood the whole body thing. Why was that so important? I just figured that for some weird reason, my dad wasn't as bored by the aimless prattle about the pageant circuit as I was. Or maybe he conquered his boredom by rotating in new women regularly.

He never really slowed down enough to get bored. Those detailed to-do lists were a testament to the hectic schedule my dad kept. He went out to dinner every night of the week with a different date, where he typically drank two or three beers or glasses of wine and stayed up past midnight. Then he got up at six the next day and worked on notes for his next class, or edited one of his manuscripts. He ran three miles every day. He swam several times a week. He traveled overseas to give talks at least once a month. He did consulting work for several law firms, calculating the projected net worth of the injured and the dead based on theoretical wages, adjusted for inflation.

The value of my father's life, though, was measured in speed, not dollars. Speed equals distance over time. My dad seemed to want to cover as much distance in as little time as possible.

He didn't like being alone, unless he was working. He didn't like to sit without doing something. He read books to fall asleep. I once watched him eat a raw papaya over a waste basket in his office, spraying juice and pulp all over his hands. He ate fast, with huge bites, staring at notes for his next class the whole time.

On his filing cabinet, there was an old-fashioned metal scale with two dishes. On the left, he'd scrawled the word "Supply" on a piece of paper, folded it, and placed it on the plate; on the right was the word "Demand." He'd grown up in the sooty working-class neighborhoods of Johnstown, Pennsylvania, and became an economist to help give poor people a voice in the callous world outside. But sometime after grad school, he changed his mind and became an advocate of capitalism. The market system was too formidable to resist, and my dad was never one to hold stubbornly to a belief or notion for the sake of consistency.

He voted for Jesse Helms and for Jesse Jackson. He was volatile and contradicted himself constantly, but he was always open to new arguments, new personalities, new movements, new ideas.

He was always looking for a new angle. He didn't slow down or compromise. He never stopped to apologize. He was a blur of motion.

AS KIDS, when we weren't boxing, we were playing "Elsa." Inspired by the movie *Born Free*, we would pretend we were lions and wrestle each other on our hands and knees. My dad would yell, "Attack!" and Laura and I would crawl very quickly toward my brother, who was also on his hands and knees. Eric would lift one arm to shove me a few feet, almost effortlessly, then he'd shove my sister a few feet. Sometimes he'd hold one of us down with one arm while he pushed the other one away. When we both looked defeated, my dad would yell, "Come back! Come back!"

It was a brutal mismatch, but, as with boxing, we went into it with a ridiculous, almost giddy sense of hope: This time, we'll take him down! We'll get him! When we hear the word "ATTACK," Laura will jump on his back and I'll knock his hands out from—

Slam! Facedown in the rug again. Ow.

It's a testament to my father's powers of persuasion that we kept up the imbalanced hand-to-hand combat sessions for years. He'd say, "Be tough! Be tough!" and I'd try hard to be tough—at least for the thirty seconds it took until I was cowering away from the fight.

As we got older, wrestling and boxing gave way to verbal sparring, in which my dad trained us to take direct confrontation in stride. While an outsider might interpret these sparring sessions as name-calling or teasing, my father's relentless provocation was tougher to categorize than that, fluctuating erratically between lighthearted prodding and merciless derision.

Sure, he wanted to prepare us to face our adversaries without fear, but more often than not he was just bored and felt like indulging his sociopathic streak. You could see it in the look on his face, eyes darting around the room, searching for something to rip to shreds. What made him shift on a dime like that, from relaxed to antsy and dissatisfied? Some piece was missing, something that might stop him from circling like a shark, something that might dampen his urge to attack.

Make some know-it-all remark, mention your plans to study gender issues or join a rock band or move in with your boyfriend—hell, mention *anything* about yourself—and my dad sunk his teeth in. Boyfriends were referred to merely as "that guy." Ideas and plans were blown out of the water in a matter of seconds.

"Why contacts?" he asked me when I ditched my glasses in eighth grade. "Do you want to be some kind of a glamour girl? That's so shallow. Don't be such a shallow dummy."

To my brother, though, he'd say, "Why don't you ask someone out on a date, Funky Winkerbean?"

His girlfriends told us how he bragged about us behind our backs. To our faces, though, he seemed to alternate between affectionate outbursts, sometimes expressed through song and dance, and vague disapproval at the odd, awkward birds we'd grown up to be. Why couldn't we be a little more like him? Smooth and talkative and garrulous and unrelenting. Why did we have to be so self-conscious? Nothing was more boring and un-forgivable to him than self-consciousness and second-guessing.

But when we were around my dad, we had no choice—merely trying to keep up with him meant taking part in his acts of civil disobedience. We skipped the long lines and sneaked in the exit doors of every exhibition at the 1982 World's Fair. I was instructed to "act young" so he could save money by ordering me a child's meal; then he'd pass me fried shrimp from the All You Can Eat buffet under the table. Everywhere we went, my dad stirred up trouble, flirted with waitresses, and loudly questioned any rule or policy that he deemed unreasonable or stupid. As a kid, my siblings and I wanted, more than anything, to go unnoticed, to keep a low profile. As long as we were with my dad, though, that was impossible.

A FEW WEEKS after I returned to San Francisco in the wake of my father's death, I talked to my mom about my dad's estate and the piles of stuff he'd left behind, most of which I hadn't had the chance to sort through or had avoided dealing with over the course of the two months I spent at home. She told me she'd managed to throw out a bunch of stuff that she knew was just taking up space. Immediately, my heart started to race.

"Like what? You'll ask before you throw anything away, right?"

"Oh, don't worry. These were just crazy old to-do lists. Stuff no one wants."

I was stunned. Those lists were the *only* things I wanted of my dad's. To me, they were proof of something, like those cave paintings. Proof of who my father was. Proof that he was busy, that he doodled, that he ate raw mangoes for lunch and swam twenty laps and caught the Duke–Maryland game last February. Proof that he charged $200 an hour for consulting and had four dates in the same week. Proof that he thought about his own mortality, that he was defensive and stubborn but still wanted input from his closest friends, from astrologers, from psychics, from me.

As my mom struggled to explain why she'd thrown away the lists—maybe they depressed her, maybe she was protecting him, maybe she was simply playing God—I couldn't speak, but a darkness took hold of me and tied my stomach in a knot. All at once I felt so heartbroken for him, this man who had so much power over me, but who I always saw as fragile anyway. He needed so much from the world, from us. He was ruled by his emotions and his impulses and his addictions and his boredom and his aggressive urges and his loneliness. I remembered how he'd bought himself a water bed with gold satin sheets on it, so insanely cheesy we said it looked like it belonged to Shaft. I remembered how he returned from a sabbatical in Hawaii wearing Hawaiian shirts with gold chains under them, until we called him "Larry," after the cheesy aging bachelor on *Three's Company.* Soon he'd start asking us, "What do you think of this shirt? It's new. What do you think? Too 'Larry'?"

I remembered the songs he sang, over and over, in his best imitation of an absurdly deep, old-fashioned, manly voice: *Oh Danny Boy, the pipes, the pipes are calling, From glen to glen, and down the mountain side!*

How could I forgive my mother, for erasing such crucial evidence of who he was? How would I ever know him now?

BUT I DID KNOW HIM. Unlike my mother, who was much more reserved and who censored herself to protect our feelings, my father never hid anything. He was unashamed of his contradictions. He was a swaggering misfit, insecure but overconfident, an outspoken outsider. He was a philanderer who was trying to reach some spiritual state of balance. His condo had burned down the year before he died, thanks to a fire started by his attic fan. As he stood by, watching it burn, he was described by a reporter as "stoical" and told the man, when asked for comment, "It's just stuff."

He wanted to achieve some higher state of being. *Float like a butterfly.* He wanted our help and our love. He wanted to get a rise out of us, to infuriate us. *Sting like a bee.*

Even though I found him exhausting, I felt lucky to have him around. Other people's dads seemed so boring and slow compared with him, the way they made the same old predictable jokes about their silly wives and silly daughters. They were big, clumsy elephants, good for an easy laugh, good for sheepishly hanging out in the background. My father was a fast-moving predator. He slid into view, mesmerized you with his merciless wit and smug candor, then he was gone.

Once, during a terrible month when he was misdiagnosed as having lung cancer, only to discover that the tumor in his lung was just a calcium deposit, he told me that he couldn't remember his mother hugging him when he was little, not even once. Even as he tormented his younger siblings, he felt invisible. He needed to make himself heard. He needed to be seen. He wanted to be sure that we saw him.

I saw him. He was impossible and horrible and magnificent, and I loved him. I loved him like a friend, like a sworn enemy, like a mother, like a patriot, like a sidekick, like a fan, like a spy, like a sister. I doubted his perception of the world and I worried about him, but I was loyal to his corrupt state. I knew that he needed me on his side. I was an enforcer of his despotic rule.

In 1995, when he got stuck, my heart got stuck, too. My life suddenly took on the same forward motion that his once had, but inside, I didn't know how I could ever leave him behind. My obnoxious boss, my court jester, my coach, my advocate, my tormentor was gone. He won't be back when springtime's in the meadow. My father, my loyal friend, my one true admirer, is gone.

7

Bobos

One day on the front steps of my elementary school, Mike Adams dryly informed me that my shoes were bobos. I was waiting for my mom to pick me up, and suddenly there he was, pointing at my shoes and laughing. In the kid parlance of the times, "bobos" were ruefully cheap shoes. Kids on the playground would sing:

Bobos, make your feet feel fine,
Bobos, cost a dollar ninety-nine!

Clearly Mike Adams was uninformed, though: My white sneakers with the little green zigzag of terry cloth were perfectly *good* shoes, and they were most certainly *not* bobos. "Oh yeah? Where did you get them?" he asked, and I snapped back with confidence, "Pic 'n' Pay!"

"*Ha*-ha! You're wearing *bobos*!" he squealed. But I assumed that everyone shopped at Pic 'n' Pay, with its long, tall rows of kids' shoes and its bins of sneakers that you could reach into and grab the size and color you wanted. "Where do *you* get your shoes?" I demanded. "Thom McAn!" Mike singsonged snottily at me, like it was the obvious answer to a teacher's painfully stupid question.

As my mom drove me home from school, I told her what Mike had said. "Thom McAn? What a joke!" she snorted. But her judgment had been called into question. I couldn't get this nagging doubt out of my head: Maybe my mom didn't know everything. Maybe she thought Thom McAn was just another stupid store, but maybe to people who *knew*, Thom McAn was a world apart from Pic 'n' Pay. After all, Thom McAn was in the mall with other fine stores like Merry Go Round and Chess King. Pic 'n' Pay was in a strip mall, next to a grocery store.

This was the first time it had occurred to me that our circumstances were anything but fortunate. We were firmly middle-class, we lived in a nice old house. We'd always had the same furniture, the same small, fuzzy black-and-white TV. We never had a dishwasher or a dryer or air-conditioning. We wore hand-me-downs and we got a few new things on Christmas and on our birthdays. I never really considered that anyone had *more* than we did—except for maybe Amy Carter, who lived in the White House, which had hundreds of rooms, many of them painted dark red or shaped like ovals or trapezoids, with lots of big bedrooms that had those frilly, canopied beds that I coveted. I was jealous of Amy Carter, sure. Who wasn't? But I had been drilled on all the poor kids starving in Africa enough to consider myself very lucky.

But when Mike Adams opened his mouth and said "bobos," I was forced to consider the fact that most of my friends had air-conditioning and clothes dryers and color TVs and cable and tons of toys and dishwashers and at least two cars in the driveway. I had always seen these things as excessive, almost tacky, but now I realized that this was my mom's doing. She convinced us that anything we wanted was bad for us: Air-conditioning made the air stale, clothes dried in the open air smelled fresher, doing the dishes was meditative and strengthened your character, and color TV and rooms full of toys were for dim-witted children.

But maybe these things meant you had plenty of money! Maybe most of my friends were rich, and we were poor. Maybe other kids looked at my family with the horror and pity with which we regarded the colonists, who, as we'd just learned in school, lived without indoor plumbing or antibiotics or toasters.

THAT SUMMER, my sister and I saw *Fiddler on the Roof* on TV, and we decided to write a musical and record it on our tape recorder. Our musical, *Rich Girl, Poor Girl*, began with a humble waif, a less pathetic version of the Little Match Girl, who scrubbed the streets every day for just enough money to buy a stale loaf of bread for dinner. Like the heroine of any fairy tale, her lot in life was deeply no-fair, made even more no-fair by the fact that she had no one to whine "No fair!" to. We knew, though, that by being denied the basic rights and entitlements of a normal child, she would develop a plucky and unflappable spirit—and a strong, lovely singing voice.

Oh, I wish I were a rich girl,
A little rich girl with flowers in my hair!
I wish I were a rich girl,
A little rich girl, without a care!

I performed the part of the poor girl—I had mastered the sugary, openhearted tone of the Disney heroine, with its exaggerated enunciations and its sweetly melodramatic lilt. In order to achieve this sound, I had to open my eyes very wide and imagine that I was the cartoon version of myself, blinking big, wet, saucer eyes and smiling with tiny pink lips.

As the poor girl is scrubbing and singing, along comes a rich girl in her magnificent carriage. This is the poor girl's Bobo Moment. All those years eating stale bread in the gutter, yet it never occurred to her to feel ashamed of her circumstances.

My sister and I had no trouble writing shrill lines for the rich girl, thanks to a lifetime of stories about evil stepsisters and nasty Nellie on *Little House on the Prairie*. Naturally she scoffs and tosses her head full of curls away from the wretched sight of the poor girl in her rags and her eighteenth-century bobos.

But then, a twist! The rich girl accidentally drops a ten-pound note on the street, and the poor girl uses it to enroll in the expensive private girls' school. The rich girl vehemently argues against the poor girl's admission—in song!

She's so fat! She's so loud!
Her head is always in a cloud!
She doesn't wash, or study hard!
Her reading books are marred!

The headmistress, who has by now become the poor girl's advocate, answers with a syncopated melody:

She'll go on a diet, she'll be so quiet!
You'd better not make it into a riot!
She'll take a bath and do her math!
She'll read The Grapes of Wrath*!*

Then they sing together, the two parts fitting together so well that Laura and I can't stop congratulating ourselves over how brilliant we are.

Even at the ages of eight and ten, wealth meant having the good taste to be thin and polite—but it also meant belonging. Once you had money, all of your unacceptable traits would melt away, whether you were overweight or merely had beat-up schoolbooks. Then the Mike Adamses of the world would never be able to point and laugh and tell you something about yourself that you didn't already know.

So the poor girl cleans up nice and goes to school, doing her math and reading *The Grapes of Wrath* and so on, and that's about the point where we started to lose interest in our story. I think we might've dreamt up a prince for the poor girl to marry along with some unpleasant fate for the rich girl, but it all seemed sort of lackluster after that. We could've learned an important lesson from this, of course: Once you have everything you've ever wanted, what then? Things get pretty boring, really. Isn't that why celebrities and the idle rich seem to live lives of vague dissatisfaction and longing? Isn't that why stars and aristocrats alike develop drug problems and spend most of their time obsessing about whether or not to change their hair color or remodel their bathrooms again?

These things didn't occur to us, plus we weren't sure we could improve on that duet between the head mistress and the rich girl. Mostly, our story revealed that *life isn't fair*, just like our mom always told us when we lamented the injustice of having to eat eggplant or rake the leaves or wait at the bus stop in the rain. Ultimately, your fate would be decided by luck—stumbling on a huge sum of cash—and by the sympathy of fairy godmother types like the headmistress. Without such an intervention, you were doomed to wander through life as a fat, loud, distracted, filthy loser with tattered schoolbooks.

AROUND THE SAME TIME, my sister and I decided to write a letter to Amy Carter. We needed to know more about what it was like to be rich and live in the White House, plus we wanted to let her know a little about ourselves. We knew so much about her, but she didn't know us at all. That didn't seem right, somehow.

> *Dear Amy Carter,*
>
> *Hi my name is Laura and my little sister's name is Heather. We live in Durham, North Carolina. What is it like to live in the White House? Do you like having a dad who is the president? Please write back!!!*
>
> *Your friends,*
> *Laura and Heather*

About a month later, we finally got a postcard in the mail, a picture of Amy Carter on the lawn in front of the White House. It said something like "Dear Friend" and "Living in the White House is fun!" We stared at her signature for a long time. Something was funny about it. Finally, we figured it out: She hadn't signed it herself, her signature was *stamped* on there!

We were livid. Amy Carter probably didn't even read our letter! What was *wrong* with her? That brat had her minions send out postcards! It was an injustice that we couldn't live with. We got more angry the more we looked at that stupid smiling picture and that stamped signature.

So my sister sat down and wrote another letter to Amy Carter, this one very different from the first:

> Dear Amy Carter,
>
> We sent you a nice letter and all you sent us was a postcard!! You didn't even sign it yourself!!! Did you even read OUR LETTER?!! Or are you just a stuck-up brat?!! I bet you have servants who do everything for you!!! Please write back!!!
>
> Sincerely,
> Laura and Heather

A month later we got another postcard, identical to the first.

We figured that we could've kept writing insulting letters and might've kept getting identical postcards back until we had a room full of them, but then we'd probably land our family on some suspected enemy-of-the-state list, which meant that spies in black vans would follow us around and take pictures of us to make sure we weren't hatching some plan to kidnap Amy Carter and torture her until she told us what it was really like to live in the White House, until she admitted that the canopy beds were nice and the huge lawn was great, but her dad was always stressed out and she almost never saw him, and her mom . . . Well, Rosalynn obviously didn't *get* her at all.

Even though we could imagine Amy Carter's life in exquisite detail, we found it seriously unnerving that she didn't even know we existed. Could we really matter so little in the world?

ONE DAY AT THE MALL, I told my mom I wanted to go to Thom McAn. I needed to experience this store firsthand, and examine its non-bobo shoes with my own eyes.

Immediately upon stepping into the spacious, carpeted confines of the store, I recognized its inherent superiority. There were several attractive displays of brown leather shoes and two salesmen in pressed suits, roaming the carpeted floors with professional smiles plastered on their faces. My mom may not have noticed, but I could clearly see that this place was a world apart from the neon lighting and industrial-tiled floors of Pic 'n' Pay.

"Hello, ma'am, can I help you with something?" a smiling young man asked my mom in the perfect open and friendly tone of the good salesman.

"We're just looking," my mom mumbled, hoping that he'd recognize her unwillingness to engage in the sort of small talk that could only lead to wanton overspending. My mom had no patience with salesmen, and felt suspicious of the endless bandying about of niceties that occurred in the South. She was from

Chicago, and when strangers chatted her up, all she could think of was how to cut the conversation short. As a girl, she looked just like a young Ann-Margret, with a great figure and blond fleecy hair and piercing blue eyes, and she could outrun every boy in the class. But right now, she needed to lose five pounds, and she didn't want anyone looking at her in the meantime. She wore old Levis and old cowboy boots and a big puffy army-surplus coat and a light pink handkerchief tied over her tightly permed hair with gigantic, tinted Barbra Streisand glasses on her face. Among the southern moms of our town, my mom stuck out like a bag lady at a debutante ball.

"Hello!" they would call out to her in the school parking lot, smiling brightly, striding toward her (no escape now!) with their white blouses and their gold Add-a-Bead necklaces and their navy-blue skirts flocked in little yellow ducks and their hair-sprayed hairdos. "Well, we have all just been *dying* to meet Heather's moth-ah! It's so nice to *fah-nally* have a chance to say hello!" "Yes, it is," my mom would reply weakly. It's so hard to catch when you don't really want the ball.

This would only make them force their mouths into even wider smiles, but you could see something change in their eyes, as they took in that crumpled, baggy jacket and that frizzy hair. Hmm. Interesting choice. A white woman in her mid-thirties, dressed just like Fidel Castro.

My mom didn't say it, but we could tell that she thought these women were a little foolish, all gussied up with nowhere to go but the country club or the mall, to talk about each other's kids all afternoon. Did these people read books? Did they do anything but shop? They were probably nice women, but they bored her to tears. Not like she thought *she* was so interesting, but still.

So my mom scoffed at the fifteen-dollar pairs of leather shoes, she dodged the suited salesmen, and after observing that a pair of lace-up Sebagos looked like "the special, orthopedic shoes they give to handicapped kids," she asked if I was ready to leave. I knew I couldn't rally her behind this place. Giving in to my demands to shop there would be like giving in to the values of these southern women, wearing their pumps and their gold chains to walk around in circles at the mall. If they thought they were better than us, that showed you how little *they* knew. My mother said that although she might *look* like a slouch to us—all kids think their mothers are sort of pathetic, right?—we couldn't see her objectively. Did she ever mention that she could outrun every boy in her class? And all of the boys had crushes on her, of course—why wouldn't they? She was faster than them. It made perfect sense. Those were crushes that meant something, too, because they were based on an actual skill, not just looks. *Anyone* could look good.

The question of whether or not these southern moms, with their big houses and color TVs and their nice cars and their heels, were *better* than us was never on the table for her. Here she was, living in a little town in the South—she was from *Chicago*, for chrissakes—and she was supposed to purchase shoes for her kid based on the whims of a bunch of housewives in North Carolina and their smart-ass, name-calling children? Never! But how do you even *begin* to explain to your kids how absurd that would be? How do you sit them down and say, "Honey, Thom McAn isn't that great, it's just a tacky shoe store in the mall. And look, Mike

Adams calls everyone a faggot because Mike Adams, with his high, lilting voice and his fixation on fashion, is . . . well, a little *different* from the other boys." How do you explain that to even *consider* molding your purchases to fit your social environment would be to tumble, head over heels, into the mire of competitive bourgeois living? My mom read *Catcher in the Rye* in the ninth grade. She had decided decades ago that she was never going to cater to the fakers and phonies of the world.

As we left Thom McAn, I glanced back at the tasteful lighting and the shiny leather shoes for respectable, upper-middle-class schoolchildren, and I felt a pang. I knew I was supposed to wear my bobos with pride and honor, strong in my faith, never falling prey to the temptation to belong, never seeking out the comfort and relative soullessness of some unassailable uniform, purchased at a premium price. I knew I was supposed to be a little Fidel Castro.

That was fine for Ann-Margret, but could I pull it off? Maybe my mom didn't have anything to prove to anyone anymore, but I still did. She wanted me to leapfrog over the bullshit of my preteen years, but she didn't have to walk into school every day and have that little bastard pointing at her bobos and cackling.

My mom was so irreproachable, so convinced that her way of thinking was the only sane way. But maybe my mom was the deluded one. Maybe those moms with their pearl necklaces knew something my mom didn't.

Of course, this is a necessary step on the path to adulthood: You wake up one morning and see your family through the eyes of a skeptical outsider. All at once your normal family seems deranged, and you're trapped in the insane asylum with them.

But when you try to tell them they're all crazy, they shake their heads and laugh at you like *you're* the crazy one.

But isn't that what crazy people do? Crazy people don't know that they're crazy—that's part of what makes them so crazy!

I didn't want to walk around feeling like an escapee from the loony bin. I wanted to fit in. And I knew I was going to have to make an effort to do it, because I *wasn't* some cartoon heroine with sweet, loving eyes who could forgive anything and anyone. I wasn't the fastest or the prettiest, like my mom was. I was just a skinny kid in bobos. My mom didn't care, and that was nice for her, but I cared. I knew I cared, and I couldn't do anything to feel differently about it.

I wanted in. Maybe those people weren't *better* than us, but they were definitely more normal than us. They matched. In the game of "Which of these things is not like the other?" it's not too hard to spot the Cuban revolutionary among the sea of southern housewives. At age ten, the primary goal is not to excel, or to rise above it. That comes later. The goal at age ten is to be normal, to fit right in, to fade into the crowd, to become invisible.

So as we left that store, I resolved that I would get my leather Thom McAn shoes, no matter what. I would save up money and buy them for myself, and if my mom didn't like it, then fine. But I would get them, and I would be the kind of kid that the southern moms smiled at without casting their eyes downward, taking note of each flaw. My reading books would *not* be marred. I would clean up nice and be quiet and charming and well dressed. I would be acceptable, and I would belong. I would get my Thom McAns. I would get them. I would. I would get them.

8

Cheer

The air was already hot and sticky in the gym on that April afternoon when every girl at Sherwood Githens Junior High School clamored in for the first day of cheerleading tryouts. We were all there—tall girls, short girls, fat girls, skinny girls, dorky girls, popular girls, happy-go-lucky girls, angry girls—all of us anxious to beat back our essential natures and follow every order with an agreeable smile, eager to bellow cliché, asinine encouragements to the teams whose success or failure we'd barely noticed before. United in our quest to gain access to the upper echelons of preteen society, we were an ungainly herd shouting in deep, imposing voices about offense or defense, throwing our arms out (*No broken wrists! No bent elbows!*), leaping into the air as if every attempted basket or fumbling move down the field made us jump for joy. The entire exercise was deeply fake and wrong and therefore the perfect training for navigating the perils of junior high school social life.

My friend Rachel and I tried out together. After we learned

the first two cheers, we went home and practiced them for hours at her house, along with our jumps and our kicks, rating each other on every move and pointing out every flaw. "Your voice should be deeper," Rachel would say solemnly, and then, "That's too deep, you sound like a drill sergeant." "You need to get that stag jump a little higher," she'd warn. Rachel was very small and skinny and had a quick mind and a habit of snorting with disgust at people who annoyed her. Rachel had bony little bird legs and knobby knees. Her elbows became overextended when she wasn't concentrating. Rachel was not exactly cheerleader material.

I didn't tell her that, though. She was my best friend, and I needed her help to make this happen for me. I needed her relentlessly critical eye, her demanding nature, to push me to the top. "No, start from the beginning," she'd insist after a particularly inadequate attempt at a cheer. "This time, don't use the freakish voice. Try to sound a little more like yourself, and watch it with the rubbery arms." I was exhausted. Left to my own devices, I would never have practiced this much. But Rachel was a perfectionist. She was ruthless in her criticisms.

And we both knew that we needed this. Because, like Cinderella and Barbie before her, in 1983 the cheerleader represented the pinnacle of femininity to every thirteen-year-old in America: She was perky, pretty, sweet, carefree, and prone to kicking up her long legs high enough to flash her girlish ass to the known universe. Yes, she was the center of attention, yet she was also quite content to stand on the sidelines, smiling and clapping and occasionally spilling over with paroxysms of unbridled enthusiasm for the sweaty boys on the field.

The cheerleader was pure magic, embodying what every impressionable, newly sexualized, awkward young girl wanted for herself. But she didn't share. She held her bubbly, confident perfection above the heads of mortal girls like a jeweled chalice, swatting away the pimply and the fat and the sullen and the lukewarm and the self-doubting with equal contempt. Trying out for cheerleading, in seventh grade, was an act of sheer self-loathing, a tedious, torturous path that inevitably ended in rejection and inconsolable weeping.

Which is probably why every girl in school tried out. Like rats who aspire to be unicorns, our preteen masochism led us to this fate. Our determination to shame and humiliate ourselves had reached its lifelong peak.

But it was obvious that cheerleading wasn't *just* an extracurricular activity or a sport, it was a path to salvation. Without cheerleading, you were just another worthless chump in a sea of nervous nobodies. You could try your best to wear the right clothes and organize your facial features to approximate the detached expression seen on the faces of the popular kids. But without cheerleading, the most you could hope for was to fade into the background and avoid being pinpointed as a notable loser.

I RECOGNIZED THIS QUICKLY on my first day of seventh grade. Before I opened those heavy double doors and saw what was inside, I had been so proud of my brand-new pink oxford shirt from Belk's and my brand-new dark blue Calvin Klein jeans and my brand-new imitation Top-Sider loafers, finally from Thom

McAn. I'd spent my formative years happily enveloped in the naive hallways of Sacred Heart Catholic School, where even the sixth-graders still brought Holly Hobbie lunch boxes to school and played kickball at recess. No one asked anyone else to "go together," a largely asexual alliance that meant you talked to each other even less than you would otherwise. In my sixth-grade class, we'd all silently agreed that going together was "gay" and we should ignore puberty for as long as possible, pretending nothing was different about the few kids who were unfortunate enough to be plagued by premature breasts or disconcerting patches of facial hair.

But I was ready to dive into a bigger pond, stocked with a whole new species of predatory fish, public and private school kids who'd been going together for *years* now. And wasn't it obvious that I should be one of the popular ones? I figured that, in my Calvin Kleins and my Thom McAns, I'd be ushered quickly into the right circle of girls.

But then I saw them, giggling and shoving each other and passing notes in the front hallway. They had good skin. They had expensive-looking haircuts. They all knew each other. I was doomed.

And as the days passed by, I saw more clearly just how screwed I was. These kids were in a whole different league from the rest of us. They lounged by the country club pool together every summer while their fathers played golf and conversed in the amiable, mellifluous tones of southern men comfortable with their place in the world. While the rest of us were raking leaves to save up for that cherished Izod shirt, those kids were on to the next big thing: Polo, or Esprit. While the rest of us were French-

kissing our pillows, those kids were riding their shiny red mopeds to one another's houses for clandestine make-out sessions in
the family den. Their dads were doctors and lawyers and busi-
nessmen, and their moms stayed at home, stocking their pantries
with Honey Nut Cheerios and Double Stuf Oreos and caramel
Kudos bars. While we mortals got hideous rashes from lathering
our faces in ten percent Clearasil, those kids were being driven
to the best dermatologists in town.

So what was I going to do, walk right up to Arden Phillips,
with her shiny, sun-bleached bob of light brown hair and her
plaid Polo button-down shirt and her brand-new tapered Hunters
Run jeans with the zippers on the bottom, and introduce myself?
Sad little geeky me, in my straight-legged Calvin Kleins that I
now saw were all wrong, completely horribly out of style, so
much so that it pained me to put them on in the morning? Me, in
my dumb oxford shirt that bloused out, starchily, when I tucked
it into my jeans? How did Arden get hers to fall flat like that?
Me, with my enormous tinted glasses, which I thought might
look like sunglasses—weren't sunglasses automatically cooler than
normal glasses?—but which I now realized made me look like a
seventy-pound, boobless version of Barbra Streisand? *I'm* going
to walk up to Arden and she's going to overlook my obvious
flaws and bring me into the fold, inviting me to the country club
for sunbathing and chicken-salad sandwiches signed to her parents' tab, then home to her house just in time for the little red
mopeds with the cute boys on them to come puttering up her
street?

Sure, I had fantasies about it, fantasies in which I looked great
and gave myself witty lines, spouted at just the right moment, to

charm Arden and her cool friends (some of whom, I noticed, weren't all that clever and would probably welcome someone who could toss a few droll zingers into the mix). Even though I wasted multiple hours constructing these fantasies, instead of providing an escape, they only made me feel more pathetic. The fact was, nothing could ever deliver me from obscurity.

Until cheerleading tryouts came around in the spring, it had never even occurred to me that I could be a cheerleader. I'd always assumed that cheerleaders, like royalty, were simply anointed by God to reign over the rest of us. But *now* I saw that once I was a cheerleader I would fit right in—how could I not? I'd be right there, with Arden and Kimberly and Kate and Ann. At such close range, I could more accurately mimic their dress, their social habits, their verbal tics. *I could become one of them.*

I would kick up my long legs high enough to flash my girlish ass to the known universe, then I'd get invited to all of the parties where they played Five Minutes in the Closet. You couldn't get a boyfriend unless you were there. It wasn't just about being *seen* as cool. It was a practical matter.

RACHEL'S MERCILESS CRITIQUES seemed to be working. Each time a new, shorter list of names was posted on the door to one of the outdoor classrooms at school, Rachel and I were still on it. Even so, we could hardly believe that we'd make the team when it was all over. Was it really possible that the two of us could be *cheerleaders*? It defied all logic. It was like imagining that we might wake up as young aristocrats one morning, after a lifetime tolerating a mundane middle-class existence.

Rachel and I had the same flavor of academic, self-righteously middle-class parents, transplanted skeptics from New York or Pennsylvania or Chicago who dressed in ten-year-old styles and drove rusty old family cars to school. Rachel was Jewish and we were Catholic, but the two groups shared a similar scrappy-outsider's kinship in Durham. The Jewish and Catholic families I knew cast a jaundiced eye on Hope Valley, where the wealthy kids lived in their big houses and the parents drove luxury cars and spent their weekends tossing back strong drinks together, comparing notes on the latest UNC game. Self-respecting Jews and Catholics lived modestly and would sooner eat live maggots than buy their kids mopeds or Polo shirts or join an all-white country club and allow their kids to charge lunch on their tabs. That was the path of provincial Waspy lightweights.

In fact, my dad considered Protestants of every stripe suspect, but the worst, as far as he was concerned, were the Presbyterians—who made up most of Hope Valley, as far as I could tell. "Presbyterians, oh, they seem so humble, with their folding chairs and their really *casual* sermons," he'd say. "Those people believe their wealth on Earth is a sign of God's divine blessing! In other words, they think because they drive BMWs, that means they're God's favorites."

Maybe *that* was where Arden's unflappable confidence came from—from the conviction that God liked her better than the rest of us. With a face and hair and a body like that, it wasn't hard to imagine. Arden took dance lessons. She moisturized her skin. She was strong and pretty and she glowed. She made the rest of us look like badly crafted rag dolls.

But Arden had something better than just God on her side:

She had a stay-at-home mom who tooled around town in a white Mercedes all day, buying trendy outfits and expensive skin creams for her. Arden's mom wasn't your typical tacky, nouveau-riche southerner, either. She had antiques and big Oriental rugs in her house. She had books by Martha Stewart before anyone else even knew who that was. Arden was trained on how to hold herself before she hit kindergarten. She didn't say stupid things or wear the wrong shoes or embarrass herself constantly. She didn't have to gather the nerve to inform her mother that *all* the girls in seventh grade were wearing bras, whether they had something to support or not. Arden's mother probably had a range of appropriate training bras selected for her in advance of this arbitrary, invisible seventh-grade deadline.

Rachel and I had to work very hard to keep up with the Ardens of the world. Instead of sitting by the pool, we lathered our bodies in sunflower oil and dragged our silver tanning blankets onto her roof, where we were sure to get the quickest tan possible—although typically we fried ourselves pinker than bacon instead. We did extra chores so we could buy those tapered, zippered jeans and ditch our uncool straight-legged ones. We learned to apply makeup and style our hair in a vacuum of advice from our mothers, who didn't like to think about fashion at all and seemed to prefer that their kids look like eight-year-olds until they graduated from high school.

But even with all of that hard work, even with all of our practice and our nitpicking and our jumping until we felt like enormous sacks of flour and we just couldn't jump anymore, it was *impossible* to imagine that we could make the cheerleading squad. The judges would see right through us. They'd know we weren't meant to wear short robin's-egg-blue skirts and white Nikes with the matching light blue swoosh on them.

And secretly, I wondered: What if I made it and Rachel didn't? I could almost pass for a buoyant, chirpy girl if I held my breath and emptied my eyes of the slightest glimmer of independent thought. But there was no way Rachel could pull off the same trick. She was snippy and impatient and totally over junior high before it even started. Yes, she wanted to be a cheerleader, for the same pragmatic reasons we all did: The cheerleaders got the guys and had all the fun. She wanted to be the one who giggled in the halls instead of grumbling. But could Rachel hide her raw disgust for everyone around her? Could she straighten those bent elbows and disguise those knobby knees?

I worried about Rachel's chances, and daydreamed about how great it would be if we both made it. But sometimes I also secretly, guiltily, hoped that I would make it and she wouldn't. I thought it might be easier to enter this new, gilded realm without her wisecracking and her eye-rolling and her weird jokes. I suspected that the other natural-born cheerleaders wouldn't *get* her. She'd be an outcast, and she might make me an outcast, too.

AT LAST, the big day came: final tryouts for the junior varsity cheerleading team. The list was down to twenty girls, and it would be cut down to a team of eight that night. Who would make the final cut? Rachel and I powered our way through each cheer and chant, jumping and shouting and punching our moves with total focus and determination. After school, we went to Rachel's house and paced and prattled nervously, then her mom drove us to Bojangle's for fried chicken, and then back to school to see the final list, which would be posted on the now-locked doors to the school. We waited in the car for it to be posted. No one else was even around. We were excited, but realistic. We couldn't both make it, could we? Were we hoping for too much?

When we spotted both of our names on the list, we screamed and jumped up and down and Rachel tossed her half-finished iced tea all over the ground, then we laughed and hugged each other, and screamed and jumped around some more. We did it! We were freed from the ranks of the invisible forever and ever and ever, Amen! Praise Yahweh! We would wear cheerleading uniforms, made just for us! We would climb to the tops of pyramids and throw our arms into the air and yell, and the world would be watching, and probably even looking up our skirts! Hallelujah! Hallelujah! Hallelujah!

"HEY, Y'ALL, I know it's early, but I want to see how *psyched* y'all are right now! Who's *fired up* out there? Show me how *totally amped* you are, everybody!"

At this, the stocky young man in red polyester short-shorts began sashaying sideways across the dew-covered lawn, waving his "spirit stick" around furiously, the signal that all three hundred or so of us teenage girls in tiny shorts and little skirts and ribboned ponytails should leap to our feet and kick up our legs and yell "Woohoo!" thus demonstrating how *totally pumped up* we were for another day of shouting and sweating and jumping around in the hundred-degree heat.

"Who's got PMA out there right now?" the peppy cheerleading professional asked us in the high-pitched bark of a Jack Russell. By "PMA" he meant "positive mental attitude," of course. Just the mention of such an important bellwether of a cheerleader's essential vitality sent the whole camp into a nearly orgasmic demonstration of their unmitigated zeal for the day ahead, with some stepping forward out of the crowd here and there to more safely complete a toe-touch or round-off back handspring without kicking someone's teeth out, with girls searching their relatively uncluttered brains for some adequate means of demonstrating just how completely *positive* and totally overwhelmingly *psyched* they all were to be there, together, trampling the dew-covered grass as one in the premature heat of a summer morning.

As I attempted a rather leaden hurkey jump in the wet grass, Rachel flashed me a dazed look that said, "How did we wander into this horrible place, and will we ever find our way home again?" In my heart I was with her, but I couldn't afford to acknowledge that now, not when I was going to have to spend another exhausting day with a good-natured smile plastered on my face, learning dorky chants and cheers with a scary stampede of mutants who'd been mascaraed and scrunchied within an inch of their lives.

Even though Rachel and I were only a few months into our deliverance from anonymity, our friendship was already starting to buckle under the strain of our new circumstances. But then, being sequestered on a local college campus in the swampy heat of July with hundreds of yelling girls with tiny blue jays and pirates meticulously painted on their cheeks had a way of splintering long-held beliefs and turning every previous frame of reference on its head.

As the cicadas hummed to us through the open windows of our dorm rooms at night, I imagined all those girls in their beds, their hair unleashed from ponytails, a whole colony of perky young nymphs who considered themselves God's chosen ones. We were sleeping in a rarefied community of vivacious princesses who'd been lording their specialness over the heads of regular, mortal girls since a very tender age. It was like being beamed onto that planet inhabited by Greek gods on *Star Trek*.

Each morning, Rachel and I would wake up at dawn in our sticky single beds, yank on some dirty blue shorts, and pull a cursory brush across our matted heads, all the while clandestinely marveling at the elaborate grooming routines and exotic beauty products of our teammates. Then we'd dash out to the lawn, where groups of girls, ponytailed and blushed to pageant standards, were already going through their respective routines or building pyramids that were not only twice as high as the pyramids we'd attempted, but *they rocked back and forth to the beat of the cheer*. Incredible, like nothing we'd ever seen before. We were as dumbstruck as African Bushmen airlifted into the center of Tokyo.

There were crappy teams there, too, of course: unwieldy groups with sloppy hair and shabby-looking uniforms, messes of bent elbows and broken wrists, letting off a cacophony of imprecise clapping and high, screechy voices instead of the drill-sergeant bellowing currently in favor. You could take one glance at these teams and conclude that either (a) they were from some backwoods place in North Carolina where the populace wore acid-washed jeans and listened to Tesla and festooned their big, teased perms with what looked like enormous plastic purple desk accessories or (b) they were from some unenlightened school where cheerleading wasn't considered cool, so they were forced to allow unattractive, uncoordinated humans among their ranks. We chuckled and whispered behind our hands at how tacky and bad these teams were, in part to soothe ourselves over the fact that we didn't have cool black-and-white uniforms like the Panthers, this utterly superior team that had tiny black paws decorating their cheeks every morning. They painted their nails black and did back handsprings as a team and built sturdy-looking pyramids that could rock or transform into other shapes, or speed down the highway, firing bullets, for all we knew.

Interestingly, Arden and Kate and Ann would join in the giggling and scoffing at the crappy squads, but then they'd shift gears and say things like, "Y'all, I feel sort of *sorry* for them." Or "Y'all, don't laugh, that's not nice. Did you see the little one on the end with the weird braids? I feel so *bad* for that girl!" Rachel and I and a few of the other girls were comfortable heaping scorn on the others, since, as ascendant middle-class nobodies, the cool kids had heaped their quiet, superior share of scorn on us. But the popular girls were more self-conscious about their contempt for the clearly inferior. After a lifetime of casually acknowledging their own obvious superiority, they knew how to sugar their remarks in a sophisticated coating of debutante charity.

As we'd line up in our correct places and try to will our fake smiles into existence, I'd marvel at just how different Arden and Kate and Ann and Kimberly were from me and Rachel. They were affectionate with one another, and shared an easy, familial rapport that reflected the fact that they'd known each other since they were little, and were raised by southern women who lived by credos like *You catch more flies with sugar!* They brushed one another's hair and gave one another hugs and made supportive comments and said "really appreciate" and "Thank you soooo much" and even "I love you," before they went to bed, all of which sounded like complete bullshit to Rachel, but which struck me as kind and loving and made me feel like I'd been raised by angry cavemen by comparison. Rachel and I had our running caustic commentary and our inside jokes, but we hardly ever hugged or talked about our feelings without self-conscious asides or self-deprecation—not that the others didn't have their share of insecure verbal tics. But they were at ease with themselves in obvious ways that we weren't.

These were the thoughts swimming through my head as the squat little man in red shorts whipped by me for the fourth or fifth time, indicating with his spirit stick that he'd deemed my team's jumping and woohooing an insufficient expression of the undeniable fired-up-ness of the moment. Up close, he looked like a floppy blond-haired version of Olympic figure skater Scott Hamilton, but with a slightly desperate look in his eyes, like someone had just set his hair on fire.

As I quickly redoubled my efforts to woohoo with more conviction, it occurred to me that this guy had adored his days as a college cheerleader so much that he'd devoted his entire life to serving the American Cheerleaders Association or the International Cheerleading Foundation or whatever important-sounding entity ran this particular summer camp. That struck me as a little sad for him, and I briefly pondered whether he knew he was gay or not. Would he find a nice lesbian wife, like my mom's obviously gay hairdresser had? Would he spend decades of his life unaware that, instead of donning scratchy shorts and foisting his rhapsodic fascism on herds of young girls, he could be sporting assless chaps and sipping really good beer and trading witty, sarcastic banter with his brethren in Chelsea or the Castro?

But whatever complicated gender-identity issues, socioeconomic influences, and elegant layers of denial happened to be in play at that moment, the mutual support and warmth of my popular teammates and this semi-regular violent outburst of rapturous enthusiasm were beginning to make me feel like I had been born on some cold, dark planet in a frigid galaxy far, far away, one ruled by self-conscious emotional midgets who thought a mumbled "Good morning" or a fumbled hug meant you were overdoing it just a little bit. I didn't want to win the spirit stick or anything stupid like that, but I *did* want a small slice of the easy affection that Arden and Kate and Ann shared, in their knowing glances, in the way they leaned in, confiding in whispers. I was an alien determined to wriggle my way in and be accepted by these strange creatures. It wasn't just about being cool. It was a practical matter.

Rachel would never understand.

"RED HOT, our team is red hot! Our team is R-E-D red, H-O-T hot, once we start we can't be stopped!"

Mrs. Francis was glaring again, her face screwed in a rictus of disapproval, her curly hair ballooning out like an ungroomed white poodle perched on her head. We weren't getting it right. The popular girls looked nice in their uniforms, but they were distracted. They felt that cheerleading was their birthright. They didn't need to practice. Some of them were dancers and gymnasts who'd taken years and years of lessons and burned out on perfectionism and competition when they were eight or nine years old. Now they could do effortless back handsprings, but mostly they stood around on the track or the benches of the gym, chatting conspiratorially.

As the fall wore on, Rachel was increasingly out of sync with the other girls. While I befriended the rest of the team, Rachel remained suspicious of them. Didn't I agree that they were a little vapid and fake? Maybe sometimes they seemed that way, but actually, I *liked* the fact that they were garrulous and confident. I didn't tell Rachel that, but as I got to know Kate and Ann and Arden better, I found myself drawn in by their good-natured ribbing and their ability to have long, relaxed conversations about whatever was on their minds. When they started inviting me over to their houses after school, we never needed to have some activity or agenda the way Rachel always did. Instead, we just stood around in Kate's kitchen, eating and talking about whatever came up. There was nowhere important to be, there were no heavy questions to tackle. Rachel's air of urgency was replaced by a comfortable, rambling atmosphere, in which I didn't have to say anything clever or try too hard.

And even though I was obviously an outsider, with a weird old house across town with laundry hanging out back and a divorced mom with a full-time job, they didn't seem to have a problem with that. If I joked about our differences, they laughed, but to them it was all just part of my charm. I was the smart one, the weird one, the funny one. They never tried to cut me down when I was showing off or acting goofy; they didn't relentlessly pick apart the things I said. They accepted me in ways that even my own family didn't always manage.

Their prim, polite southern mothers may have struck me as cartoonishly demure at first, but not only had they managed to impress upon their daughters the importance of being accepting and encouraging above all else—traits that I was starting to see clearly had benefits—but they had accepted me, too. When I said something a little bit odd or even outrageous, they giggled wickedly. "Oh, Heathah, you ah *baaaad*," Ann's mom would coo when I stepped over some invisible line I didn't know existed. If she thought I was a freak, she had the good graces to keep it to herself. And at age sixteen, what more can you ask for?

When Rachel and I both didn't make the cheerleading team our junior year in high school, thanks in part to our growing ambivalence about the endless practices and our unremitting hatred of our cheerleading coach, we might have bonded over leaving the whole thing far behind, but instead our friendship started to fall apart. I was still close friends with the cheerleaders, while Rachel started spending more time with the alternative crowd.

Sure, I tended to feel like the most sharp-tongued, neurotic member of my circle, but around Rachel I just felt like a dim-witted rube. She refused to hide her increasing exasperation with me. I knew Rachel wasn't a mean person, but my insistence on straddling two worlds seriously pissed her off. In high school, you weren't allowed to be two things at once. You couldn't hang out with two different groups, claiming equal allegiance to both. You had to choose sides.

THE CHEERLEADER is a natural villain. She's so easy to revile, in her silly little outfit, watching the game with unseeing eyes, baking cookies for the team like a spineless housewife in training. One look at the dumb pigtails and the pom-poms and that air of pert self-possession and it's almost impossible *not* to root against such a creature.

We want the cheerleader to end up humiliated or dumped. We'd like to find out that she has an eating disorder, or that she was molested by her uncle, anything to reveal that she's just as insecure as the rest of us, anything to either exact the vengeance of a thousand uncoordinated plain Janes, or to transform the chirpy little bitch into something resembling a sympathetic character.

This is the part of the story where I should recognize some essential flaw in my upper-middle-class, lily-white, privileged southern friends, with their absurd debutante balls and their cloistered social circles and their chuckling, old-fashioned fathers and idle, materialistic mothers. This is where I should realize that Rachel and I were natural allies and friends. Rachel, the plucky, clever underdog, is obviously destined to be the hero of this story.

But real life is never as cleanly dissected into good guys and bad guys. In the end, I chose Kate and Arden and Ann. I chose their warmth and their ease with one another and their affection-ate teasing. We had fights and misunderstandings and breakups and makeups, but over the long haul, those were my real friends. Even though I wore the wrong shoes and laughed too loud or got flustered and said something dumb, they didn't try to mold me to match them. They liked me just the way I was. I never would have predicted it, not for a minute.

9

With or Without You

In the fifth grade, I made an ashtray out of clay and painted "I ♥ Harrison" on it in bright red letters. I had never met Harrison Ford, and I didn't smoke. But to a budding romantic, the facts are irrelevant. Reality is something the young romantic molds like clay, to fit his or her particular emotional needs at the time.

In my malleable internal world, Harrison Ford was destined to be mine. Of course he was exactly like Han Solo, the devil-may-care captain of the *Millennium Falcon* he played in *Star Wars*: reckless and charming, but a little bit vulnerable when things didn't go his way. Anyone could see that Carrie Fisher wasn't really his type—too bossy and cold—but he would definitely fall madly in love with me, a ten-year-old girl with gum stuck in her hair. Sure, I was a little young for him, but that didn't make him a pedophile or anything. When we finally met—maybe I'd go to the *Empire Strikes Back* premiere and he'd spot me behind the velvet rope—he'd immediately recognize that we were *soul mates*, destined to be together forever and ever. When he looked into my eyes, he would fall into a trance, just like the prince in *Cinderella*. And then, of course, he'd wait around for eight or nine years, until I was old enough to marry him and move into his gigantic house and stuff.

I thought about Harrison Ford a lot back then. When my parents were fighting or my sister was being a jerk or when nothing at all was happening, when I was just alone in my room, bored, lying on my bed and staring at the trees blowing in the breeze outside my window, I would think about him. Mostly I would think about how *amazing* it would be once we finally met, how he would sit on the olive, wall-to-wall shag carpeting in my room, his chin on his knees, and stare into my eyes for hours, marveling at how unbelievably interesting and mesmerizingly beautiful and unnervingly funny I was. He wouldn't be able to take his eyes off me, he would just be so *overwhelmed* by his good fortune at finding such a brilliant, pretty, smart . . . ten-year-old with gum stuck in her hair.

He would quickly forget all about his busy and important life as an actor, of course. Who cared about any of that, really, when he could be with me instead? He would listen to all of my crazy ideas (but he wouldn't think they were crazy at all, they would make *total* sense to him!) and every now and then he'd interrupt me to say something like "Oh my God, you are just *incredible*." Or "Did you know that your eyes almost look green in this light?"

Man, it would be so great to have him here, I'd think. *If only he were here right now!* Everything would be perfect. Sometimes we would go for walks together, holding hands. Maybe he would take a break to work in his wood shop occasionally. (Before he became an actor he was a carpenter, you know. *Just like Jesus*.). But mostly, he would just listen.

I had so much to tell him.

SOMETIME IN THE MIDDLE of March, I start showing up for biology class early so I can get a good view. They're both on the second lunch period, so they walk to the cafeteria a few feet from the window where I sit. They can't see me, thanks to the glare of midday sun on the glass (I've gone outside and checked), so I'm free to study them both carefully—how he puts his hand on the small of her back as they walk together, as if he's guiding her, or how, on other days, their fingers interlace loosely, like they've been together for years. Sometimes they stop and talk to his friends, laughing together and smiling and then moving on, always touching.

I evaluate her style choices: jeans today, and that awful Cosby sweater again, the one with the big red square and the blue circle on it. Her hair is in a French braid with a red ribbon at the end today, but on most days her hair hangs down to the middle of her back in an impossibly thick tangle of curls the color of daffodils. With no visible roots, the color *must* be natural. And her eyes! Big, aqua-blue gems outlined in heavy black eyeliner. Those *have* to be colored contacts. Every day, she's got on layers of thick mascara and foundation and blush, carefully applied. But why not? When you're six feet tall and blond and have enormous blue eyes that look like they're lit from inside your head, you might as well flaunt it, until you're towering above the mortals around you like a gigantic malevolent baby doll, carelessly crushing innocent hearts in your pretty white porcelain hands.

Carla Jean Hill, living doll, goddess Godzilla. Carla Jean Hill, my nemesis, former friend and current girlfriend of my very first boyfriend ever, Mark Fisher. Carla Jean Hill bestrides the narrow world of Charles E. Jordan High School like a colossus.

A few weeks ago, she was just Mark's friend, the one who was really pretty and made him laugh, sure, but she would never deign to go out with him. Yeah, she'd whip up batches of frozen margaritas for him on weekends when her mom was out of town. And she *did* seem a little bit sulky over the past few months since Mark and I started dating, batting her long eyelashes sadly at him, willing him to understand something she wouldn't put into words. Mark could tell you himself, she *was* awesome—just really funny and super cool and lots of fun—but she'd *never* go out with him, not in a million years.

That was how he reassured me. Not by saying, "Oh, Carla, no way. She's not nearly as cool as you!" Not with a "Carla? Are you kidding? She's like my sister!" No. It was: "Oh, Carla, we're just friends. She would never go out with me. She dates, like, older guys, guys with their own apartments. Guys with *mustaches*."

There's nothing quite like being totally overmatched and knowing it. Like a field mouse facing a street fight with a foot-long city rat, my fate was completely out of my control. All I could do was close my eyes and hope for the best.

I didn't even look for reassurance from Mark. *But what if she secretly likes you?* Even when he told me that Carla had broken up with Mr. Mustache, I was worried, but I never said a word. *You'll never dump me to go out with her, will you?* I didn't want to know.

Mark and Carla were both seniors. I was just a sophomore, one with stringy brown hair and brown eyes. Next to Carla's Superstar Barbie, I was a flat-haired, flat-chested, flat-footed Skipper doll. Poor awkward Skipper, with her bad bangs and that pathetic hopeful look plastered on her face. *"Can I come, Barbie? Can I? Can I?"* you could practically hear her whine, but you just *knew* that Barbie wouldn't dream of it. *"Maybe next time, hon!"* she'd chirp lightly as Ken's Corvette growled predatorily outside. Then she'd tiptoe out the door, leaving Skipper to weep into her hands, knowing that she'd never have big boobs or a Dream House or elbows that bend.

That's how I felt the first time I saw Mark and Carla together, through the window in that biology classroom. I put my head down on my desk and sobbed. Mark had dumped me just two weeks earlier, saying he wanted to spend more time with his friends. By "friends" he had clearly meant his *friend*—you know, the six-foot-tall blue-eyed blonde? I felt sick. My arms formed a steamy terrarium around my head as my tears and snot dripped all over the desk and my face. I had seen this coming, but I still couldn't believe it: Mark was with Carla! Now I would *never* get him back! Now we would never get married and have lots of kids and move to Greensboro together!

This was 1986, a year that started as a rainbow-filled day-dream of true love, and ended in darkness and disgrace. Once I got older, of course, I knew that heartbreak was nothing special, as predictable as rain. Heartbreak took so many forms and wore so many faces over the years to come that eventually I started to tackle it with a practiced, almost professional manner. Ah yes, here we go again: the crying and the accusations, the snotty tissues making a graceful arc toward the nearest waste-basket, the hopeless calls, asking for further explanation. *Why? But I thought we were in love!* And then, the long days in bed, star-ing at the ceiling, wondering what I did wrong, wondering how I'd ever make it through life without him. And after that? The weight loss. The aimless sulking. The reading of New Age tomes about listening to your calling instead of mooning over guys, books about honoring your *soul* and *spirit*, a solemn, solitary pro-cess that involves lots of aerobic exercise and low-fat diets and pedicures.

But in 1986, I'd never known heartbreak before. In 1986, heart-break drove a canary-yellow '78 Pinto with The Who's "Baba O'Riley" playing in the tape deck. Heartbreak looked just like Damone from *Fast Times at Ridgemont High*. Heartbreak held my hand in the hallways at school and bought me fries at Hardee's and drove me to all the best senior parties and thought I was smart because I used polysyllabic words like "ambivalent." Heartbreak played the drums in the marching band and quoted Pee-wee Herman liberally, even as he was breaking up with me. What had he said? "You don't want to get involved with a guy like me. I'm a loner, Dottie. A rebel." He giggled at his own joke, then saw the look on my face and corrected course. "No, but seriously, I'm a senior now, and . . ."

In 1986, I fell in love with Mark Fisher, and then, after it was over, I fell in love with heartbreak itself. I wallowed and wept and wondered what he was doing *right now*. Eventually, the point wasn't that Mark and I should be together, it was the fact that *cruel fate was keeping us apart*. Mark and Carla were just sup-porting characters in my own private romantic movie. I was the star, the tragic heroine, the crestfallen but pure-hearted ingenue, the one whose eyes almost look green in this light.

FOR MY THIRTY-NINTH BIRTHDAY, my two-year-old daughter picked out a card for me that came in an envelope with a shiny pink castle and a rainbow on it. When I opened the envelope, a trumpet sounded, followed by a voice that said, "I now pronounce you *the most beautiful birthday princess in all the land!*"

All I could think was, *Well, it's about fucking time.*

There was no prince on the envelope or on the card. At least when you're very little everyone is willing to acknowledge just how irrelevant he is.

THE FIRST TIME you fall in love, it's like throwing a party in your head and no one else is invited, a party where they play nothing but "Don't You Forget About Me" over and over again. The actual particulars—driving to Hardee's in a beat-up yellow Pinto, your thighs sweating into the torn black upholstery of the passenger seat, your mind searching for something clever to say—aren't all that compelling. When you're with the object of your desire, it's not very enjoyable: You're paralyzed by fear. You can hardly breathe. Did you laugh too loud just then? Was that stupid to say? Is there something stuck between your teeth? Are your armpits wet? Does your breath smell terrible? Does your hair look bad?

The real enjoyment of young love happens when your sweetheart isn't around. That's when he gets to be the enthralled, love-struck man of your dreams, and you (the real star) get to be transfixing and beautiful and perfect. In the luxury of solitude, in the gentle folds of a fertile young imagination, fear and self-doubt and sweaty palms and halitosis give way to a shiny, sparkling dream girl with witty remarks tripping off her minty tongue.

But I was more than ready to cultivate a rich fantasy world around the first mildly interested mortal to wander into my crosshairs. By the time I met Mark, I had been mooning over imaginary boyfriends for almost a decade. In the second grade I had a heart-stopping crush on Tim Rawlins, who I was sure would love me dearly once I gathered the courage to speak to him. In the third grade, I gave David Hernandez a card with a traced Ziggy on the front, then crept off to the girls' bathroom to cry for twenty minutes from an immediate rush of regret and embarrassment. In the fourth grade, every time I heard "Just When I Needed You Most" by Randy VanWarmer, I would grow quiet and daydream about Derek Jacobs, who'd graduated from the sixth grade the year before, heartlessly leaving me to face elementary school all alone. In fifth grade there was Harrison Ford, perhaps my most practical choice of boyfriend up to that point, seeing as he spoke in complete sentences and appeared capable of discussing subjects outside of Something Funny That Happened on the Kickball Field Today and Stuff That's Gross.

But practical choices were beside the point. The real human beings I targeted only served as visual inspiration for my extravagant daydreams, like pornography. All I wanted was to play with made-up versions of Tim Rawlins and David Hernandez and Harrison Ford in my head, to move them around like Ken dolls and give them charming things to say, mostly about how great I was.

Without the escape of these daydreams, how else could I have endured the mundane torture of having no control over my life or my circumstances? I was lonely. I had no one to talk to. My parents didn't really listen or understand. My friends were too wrapped up in their own dramas to care that much about mine. How could I have survived, without the solace of a robust imagination?

When my father picked me up from a beach trip with my friend Louise so we could drive across the country to take Eric to college, I probably listened to "Tea in the Sahara" by the Police over a hundred times on my Walkman. This melancholy song perfectly captured my deep and abiding love for Jay (last name unknown); see also: some sixteen-year-old guy Louise and I had stood around giggling at for two days straight. He and his friend (not nearly as cute, name unimportant) couldn't find any girls their age to hang out with that week, so they were forced to spend time with two fourteen-year-olds. "*Thank you, God*, for keeping the older chicks away this week!" Louise had gushed after we met Jay for the first time. Love, for us, was a matter of opportunity and blind luck. Skipper doesn't mind that Ken is talking only to her because Barbie is busy with G.I. Joe. Skipper is just amazed at her good fortune—and hoping against hope that Ken doesn't notice that her elbows don't bend.

As I said good-bye to Louise and drove away with my dad, I didn't need to get to know Jay any better. I just needed a way to survive three weeks in the car with my dad, my sister, my brother, and my dad's girlfriend, Brandy, without losing my mind. Instead of bickering with Laura and Eric and wanting to punch Brandy in the face for stealing gum out of my purse, I put on my headphones and stared out the window and pictured walking across the beach on an overcast day, searching for Jay, my one true love. Or, if I was in a little bit better mood, I'd listen to "The Tide Is High" by Blondie or "Missing You" by John Waite.

Once I found a love object to focus on, the unspeakably sad, indistinct, creeping form of melancholy I was haunted by as a kid became a sugary, glowing daydream with a pop-ballad soundtrack. Love transformed loneliness from a static state of depression to an extended, self-aggrandizing trip into the glossiest reaches of my imagination. Spurred on by love songs and *Sixteen Candles*, loneliness went from feeling lonely to feeling transcendent.

It's no surprise that by the time Mark Fisher entered the picture, most of what I loved about being his girlfriend was created in the glittery bubble of my imagination. To him, we were just hanging out and eating fries on weekends, punctuated by a little light groping. But in the dreamland of my head, we were the windswept stars of an extra-long Duran Duran video. When he dumped me, the biggest loss wasn't that I couldn't spend time with him anymore, it was that I was no longer special, no longer a star, and I had no excuse to wander around in a daze, sighing deeply.

But then Mark and Carla appeared around school together, and I saw that my role had become more demanding, more complex. As the rejected ex, I was arguably more special than ever. After all, those two were *happy*. Who cares about happy couples? They're boring. That's why the movie ends right after the star-crossed lovers finally embrace: The second they find love, they don't really matter anymore. The camera loses interest in them and moves on.

But it lingers . . . on that girl over there, the one whose heart just got shattered into a million pieces! Look how she suffers! She'll never be the same. *She deserves so much more.* She's been unfairly persecuted, but anyone can see, in the soulfulness reflected in those sad eyes, that *she* is the special one! Somehow her little flaws only make her all the more lovable (unlike that big, obvious, blond baby doll of a girl, with eyes the eerie aqua blue of the water at miniature golf courses).

When we're young, we cope with loneliness by creating love out of thin air, by making it oversized and dramatic, by placing better versions of ourselves at the center of it. But when we actually fall in love, it pales in comparison with the movie in our heads—at least until our hearts are broken. Then things get colorful again. Eventually, heartbreak starts to feel a little more romantic than actually being in love. Being lonely begins to feel more vivid and exciting than being with someone. Unless, of course, we find someone who makes us feel lonely and rejected all the time. That kind of love is almost as romantic as heartbreak.

Because who knows how to sit and appreciate someone else in the moment? Who isn't trapped inside their own neurotic head, their palms sweating, more anxious to impress than to listen? Real friendship, real intimacy, comfort in the company of another human being, the things that *real* love—love that's richer and deeper than a romantic fantasy—is based on: Who knows how to achieve such impossible feats when young? Where would I have learned such exotic skills? Maybe from the squirrels nesting outside my window. Maybe from the storybooks on my shelves, about the Little Fur Family, warm as toast, smaller than most. Not from my siblings. Not from my parents. We were the Little Brute Family, known to wear hobnailed boots and to kick people, hard, when things didn't go our way.

I soothed my lonely heart with glorious visions of a love that would save me, set to a Blondie soundtrack. By falling in love with love itself—invented, magical, fleeting, glorious, imaginary love—I prepared myself to spend my life alone. By turning loneliness into romantic longing, I gave my empty life a purpose. I wrote dreary little love songs on my guitar, songs I sang in a sad voice. Nothing was better than the sweet melancholy of longing. I savored it for years. Nothing else came close to mattering as much.

But who could possibly live up to such mournful songs or to decades of perfectly honed fantasies? They don't call it the greatest love of all for nothing: In our daydreams we're adored and cherished, and everything we say matters. When love comes along, it feels awkward and ineloquent and clumsy and mundane by comparison. The only princes who keep our attention are the ones who are about to disappear over the horizon.

NOW THAT I'M OLDER and (theoretically) wiser, I'm a little nostalgic for the feeling that love might sweep me into a new, entirely different reality. I miss the belief that I won't have to lift a finger to save myself, that someone will come along and make everything simple and easy. It would be nice to feel that every little idea that flickers through my head matters *desperately*, that I *need* to share it, that I have *so much* to tell some imaginary prince.

But I wouldn't trade that feeling for what's real—this little house where my husband and I bustle past each other, trying to keep the dogs from barking or the baby from crying, these small rooms where we vacuum and cook and paint little toenails and read stories and shower and grimace and roll our eyes and sing songs and bicker and sigh and sleep like stones. When friends lament the fact that the magic is gone from their marriages, I wonder about the value of magic, compared with the value of feeling accepted and understood, at long last. Each day my husband and I work elbow to elbow in our little factory, sweating and gritting our teeth and trying to remain calm as someone spills their juice or the dogs hurl themselves at the front windows to ward off stray cats. There is no magic, but if there were, we'd use it for something practical, like cleaning the dog hair off the rug. We don't gaze into each other's eyes. We quickly do dishes and straighten up and check e-mail and fold laundry and ignore the phone. We do smile at each other every now and then, when someone says something ridiculous or clever or someone cleans the kitchen floor unexpectedly or brings home a block of really good cheese.

There is no time for love songs, but we know each other well. He is absentminded and defensive and funny and his eyes almost look green in this light. I am overly critical and distracted and unbearable, and I am the most beautiful birthday princess in all the land.

10

The Toad *Work*

Why should I let the toad *work*
Squat on my life?
                    —Philip Larkin

The fifth time you hear "Papa Was a Rolling Stone" in the course of two hours, some central switch in your brain is flipped. Triggered by unwelcome, repetitive stimuli, a sensor deep within your gray matter assumes that either you've been sent to Guantánamo or you've wandered into an outdoor mall and can't find your way out. Your nervous system soon down-shifts in an attempt to protect you from the traumas to follow, whether it be waterboarding, roach-infested gruel, or a fountain that's about to make streams of water dance to "I'm Your Lady" by Céline Dion.

I can only assume that this altered state of consciousness protected me from long-term post-traumatic side effects that might've otherwise arisen in the wake of my brief tenure as sales

associate at the Gap, an experience that mental-health profes-
sionals have since classified as roughly equivalent to three years of
breaking up rocks in Mongolia. Apparently, few humans maintain their sanity when subjected to a repeating loop of upbeat
corporate-approved soul tunes while "straightening the north
wall"—as my supervisor, Olivia, instructed me to do, over and
over again, during that dark time—without a compensatory ad-
justment to the frontal lobes, one that, thankfully, dampens the
urge to strike said supervisor in the knees with the nearest
Plexiglas folding board.

Folding boards are the waterboards of the Gap indoctrination
process. Used to ensure that every single item of Gap clothing is
folded to the proper dimensions, thereby producing perfectly
aligned, color-coordinated stacks of clothing against every wall,
folding boards are whipped out every time employees might
otherwise have an idle second or two in which to indulge their
own unsanctioned, noncommercial, independent flights of fancy.

My stint at the Gap occurred well before it came to symbolize
the homogenization of American culture. The Gap had no celebrity spokesmodels, and had yet to take over huge tracts of mall
territory. Back then, it was just a place to get pocket T's and
cheap jeans, and most stores were no bigger than your average
Orange Julius. As a result, the clothing was stacked in towering
piles, a setup that required customers to unfold and rumple giant
mounds of clothing as they moved along, typically while a disapproving sales associate stood by impatiently with a folding
board, anxious to swoop in and restore order to the universe.

It was a losing battle. This might explain why my supervisor,
Olivia, always had a stubborn edge to her voice, a flinty, merci-

less tone that made it clear to me that, while straightening the north wall might *seem* like a tedious and trivial task, anyone with a solid background in retail (which I so obviously lacked) could see that it was an important job, and one to be completed with the utmost professionalism. Even when the store was empty and the north wall looked, to my eye, flawlessly organized, each T-shirt or cotton cable-knit sweater folded, flat and perfectly aligned on top of the next, Olivia saw utter chaos.

Or maybe Olivia's tone arose from her life outside those three navigationally precise but disorienting walls. Within hours of starting my first shift, Olivia informed me, unprompted, that she'd been a student at Wake Forest just a few years prior, but things had gone wrong, *horribly wrong*, which should clarify why an obviously smart woman like her was stuck here, in the mall, trying to teach spoiled brats like me the art of retail. Olivia had been applying to law schools when she became pregnant. Her asshole boyfriend wanted nothing to do with his kid, you see, and her parents (also assholes) were no help at all, so she was forced to drop out of school and raise the little asshole all by herself, all the while assuming a full-time managerial position just to make ends meet.

Olivia told me these things not with a casual, "by the way" tone, nor with a spirit of friendliness or camaraderie. Her brow was furrowed as if it *pained* her to explain herself to me, yet it was imperative that she do so. Even when she showed me wallet-size photos of her kid, she did so unsmilingly, as if she were sharing pictures of a cancerous tumor removed from her body months earlier.

I got it. She was just like me, happy and naive, everything was coming up roses, and then a bunch of assholes conspired to ruin her entire life. Recognizing this, I should respect her *and* her position of authority—you know, to make up for the lack of respect she had for either.

Even though I found her sour and humorless, I still felt a little sorry for Olivia. There was much anger in her! She obviously didn't like being a mother. Maybe she was still furious at her ex-boyfriend—wherever he laid his hat *was* his home, after all. Either way, her self-esteem clearly took a big hit every time she encouraged me, with a straight face, to "get the customer into our Gap jean," even if the customer asked *specifically* to see the Levi's. And each time she chirped, through a forced smile, "How about a pair of socks to match that sweater?" I was embarrassed for her.

Olivia was less merciful when it came to her charges. One afternoon I was straightening the west wall when a suspicious character entered the store. Even though I had been warned, very specifically, to watch out for angry women who lug around big tote bags while avoiding all eye contact, at that moment, my mind was grinding along in a very low gear. As I tweaked the corners of an already-immaculate pile of Gap acid-wash jeans, a very large, pissed-off-looking black woman with an enormous bag on her shoulder was wandering around the store, glaring as she rifled through the clothing.

My fellow sales associate, Carol, a quiet black woman in her mid-forties who'd been working for Olivia for over a year, abandoned her folding post and materialized a few inches from my ear. "I think that woman is *stealing!*" she whispered. I looked up from my pile of jeans.

"That's not good," I said flatly. Couldn't she see I was busy?

"We need to *do something!*" she said, eyeing the woman nervously.

I just looked at Carol. She really wanted *me*, a skinny sixteen-year-old white girl, to walk up and tap this woman on the shoulder and basically call her a *criminal*, then smile and wait for her four-inch jewel-encrusted nails to tear my face in half for being such a presumptuous, stuck-up, racist bitch?

Since I *was* enough of a presumptuous, stuck-up, racist bitch to believe that (a) the woman was shoplifting and (b) she would probably assault me for saying so, I probably deserved to have my face torn in half. But I wasn't about to offer myself up for that kind of punishment, so I returned to my folding, glancing up now and then to see if Carol was going to gather the courage to confront the woman. She didn't.

During my next shift, Olivia pulled me aside and said that we needed to talk. "Carol told me that this woman was shoplifting and *you didn't even notice.*"

"That's right. I was folding some stuff and Carol was right there and *she noticed first.*"

"You're *always* supposed to have your eyes on the floor! She also said that you didn't speak to the woman or do anything to stop the situation."

"No, I didn't." Could she be serious? The timid teenager is in charge of store security, while the experienced retail professional is in charge of what? Tattling?

"This is your first warning. You need to keep your attention on the customers *at all times.*"

Aha, I thought. *Olivia wants to fire me!* Even though I felt

annoyed by this injustice, I also found it oddly soothing, because it meant that I really *didn't* belong among the surly assistant
brand-experience experts and customer-service associates of this
strange never-never land, smiling through clenched teeth under
a rainbow of pocket T's.

OUR FIRST JOBS teach us the value of work—or, rather, that in this
modern age work has almost no value whatsoever. Mostly we
learn just how screwed we'll be if, down the road, we have the
misfortune of *actually having to work for a living*—you know, *real
work*, digging ditches or flipping burgers or folding sweaters for
hours on end.

Not that I didn't know how to do hard work by then. My
mom was a firm believer in backbreaking labor as a cure for whatever ails you, whether it be an unfocused, free-floating angst or
a growing frustration with the unbroken monotony of domestic
imprisonment that passes for childhood. The whiny declaration,
"Mommy, I'm *borrrrred!*" translated roughly for my mom as,
"Mother, I require the structure of several hours of scrubbing
radiators with a wire brush to make me once again appreciate the
sheer joy of being alive."

And as oppressive and difficult as the work she gave me was—
priming and painting doors, scrubbing bathtubs, raking leaves—I
always got into the groove eventually. I would enter a meditative
state and train my full attention on figuring out the most efficient way to paint an old paneled wood door without leaving
tacky paint streaks behind, or deducing the fastest way to remove
thick ivy from a square foot of backyard. I refused to be discour-

aged by sore arms or spilled paint. I shook off the feeling that there were bugs crawling all over me (in North Carolina, in the heat of summer, there usually were). I took no small amount of pride in my talent for trimming bushes and sweeping driveways, probably because my mom, recognizing how easily I could be manipulated by my hungry ego, flattered me into thinking I was some sort of unheralded housework champion.

But better than the work itself, there was the satisfaction of *having worked*. I loved peeling off filthy layers of clothes and sinking into a hot bath, my arms aching. I felt important, vital to the smooth functioning of the household. My value could be seen in the clean borders of trimmed ivy or the shine of a freshly painted wall. I assumed that most kids my age were complete wimps compared with me. Their dads did all the hard household tasks. But my dad had a condo across town ("No more working in the yard!" he'd smugly told us when he bought the place) and my mom already had a full-time job. It was up to me to make things look nice.

The work I did at my first few crappy jobs shared none of the benefits of the work I'd done at home. Crappy jobs weren't remotely meditative or satisfying, as it turned out. There were too many irritating coworkers or customers around at all times to achieve anything approaching a Zen state of mind, and there were rarely any concrete accomplishments to take pride in. Even if you completed some clear task—folding a pile of long-sleeved pocket T's, using the carpet sweeper on the bread crumbs by the bar, making all the five-dollar bills in the cash register face the same way—chances are some bumbling coworker would come by and undo your work in a matter of minutes. Your extra efforts went unnoticed by your sullen supervisors, the fruits of your labor vanished into thin air, and the government greedily snatched up a shocking chunk of your already measly paycheck. Sadly, menial jobs seemed to be about showing up with a smile on your face, appearing busy, not making any unnecessary waves, and ducking out the second your shift was over.

NO ONE DEMONSTRATED the proper skepticism with which to approach a menial job better than Lance, my assistant manager at Barney's Ice Cream. Lance was in his early thirties but still lived at home with his parents. Although they weren't technically assholes like Olivia's parents, they *were* constantly on Lance's case about moving out. But Lance needed to save a little more money before he could do that. Money for rent, plus some money to get a few (somewhat vague but nonetheless very important) projects off the ground.

Every time we worked together, Lance not only refused to fulfill his duties as assistant manager, but also cast aspersions on my wishes to fulfill *my* duties as ice cream scooper. He grew impatient with any side work that might stand in the way of my ability to chat aimlessly with him for hours on end. "Don't wash those scoops out, leave that for the morning shift," he'd say, or, "Sure, we're *supposed* to mop the floor when we close, but frankly, my dear, I *could give a shit!* Just wet that bitch down and call it a night."

Since he made it nearly impossible for me to get any work done, the two of us spent most of our time eating ice cream and gossiping about the other managers and cashiers. Lance hated the store's main manager because she was (according to Lance) moody, ugly, and a redneck. He also disliked the owner, because he was "like, *old* and shit."

Lance's other favorite activities included (a) complaining about his nagging parents, (b) making fun of how customers looked, dressed, or talked, and (c) telling bad jokes and then laughing at them, really loudly, for a long time. Although he might've struck me as impossibly negative at some other time in my life, I was in high school then, so Lance was just my speed.

One afternoon, Lance confessed to me that his parents had forced him to take the job at Barney's, but he was *really* a fashion designer. He designed these baggy jeans for women, jeans that folded over at the top and were cinched with a belt, jeans that were totally cool and hip and just *wild*. Once I saw his prototype—which he still needed to find a seamstress to make but which he *knew* would look fantastic on any woman (myself included)—I would see that they were an instant trend poised to sweep the globe.

As I pondered the likelihood of feeling that way about *any* pair of baggy jeans, let alone a pair of baggy jeans designed by a guy who had a Jheri-curled mullet just like Lionel Richie's, the phone rang.

"Yes. I'm the manager. Yeah. Oh." Long pause. "Right. Okay. I'm sorry that you feel that way. Yep. Mmm. All right. Bye."

Lance came back to where I was standing. "You know, Heather, some people are so full of shit, *you can smell it on their breath through the telephone!*"

"Who was that?"

"Some bitch going on about a fly in her chicken-salad sandwich and how, when she showed it to some 'young man' here, he picked it out without hardly apologizing or nothing. She was just *outraged*, you know, just so *offended* and *appalled*! Like she had something stuck up her butt, you know what I'm sayin'?"

"*Was* there a fly?"

"I don't know. Yeah. But it was tiny, like you could hardly *see* it. I wanted to say, Bitch, I can't keep the flies from your fuckin' sandwich! Flies are gonna do what flies *do*!"

On another slow afternoon, Lance told me that his parents had forced him to take the job, but he was *really* a songwriter. He then pulled a glossy, folded bit of music out of his duffel bag. On the cover there was a couple walking on the beach under the words "Cherished Memories." This was Lance's song, one that got published by a real, live *music publishing company*.

I stared at the pages, in shock. "Wow, that's great, Lance! How did you get in touch with this company? Did they just love it so much when you played it for them that they decided to publish it?"

"No, I just sent them the music, and I guess it *moved* them. You know?"

"So who's going to record it?"

"Well, now that it's published, *anyone* could perform it. I think Dionne Warwick would love it. It fits her voice, you know?"

I stared hard at the notes and the lyrics on the page. Something about a sunset fading from pink to gold to blue. Lots of ellipses.

Suddenly I felt really stupid. Lance must have *paid* some company to print his song on a piece of paper! Lance was a dreamer.

I felt terrible. I had never considered anyone in his position before. This was before shows like *American Idol* brought a teeming universe of deluded, largely untalented wannabes to the public's attention. Sure, I knew that not everyone grew up with the same opportunities and privileges, but that usually began and ended with starving children in Ethiopia. It had never occurred to me that there were scores of people just like Lance, who had big dreams that would never come true, *and they didn't even know it.*

Lance seemed so sad to me then, I could hardly stand it. I hated thinking about him, wasting the rest of his life working at Barney's and sleeping in his parents' den, just so he could spend every free minute writing bad love songs or designing terrible jeans. Why hadn't anyone told him that he'd never make it big with these things? Why couldn't someone snap him out of it, and make him face reality? But then, would he really get a chance at happiness once he knew the truth, or would knowing the truth ruin his only chance at happiness?

Lance demonstrated just where a combination of creativity, a rebellious spirit, and thinking outside the box might lead me: nowhere. As far as I could tell, dreaming great big dreams was a great big mistake. No, the real goal in life should be, first, to move out of your parents' house, then, to find some very practical way to avoid real work at all costs.

"WOULD YOU EVER SLEEP ON THE JOB?" The balding manager behind the desk smiled slightly when he asked me this, as if he knew the question was absurd for a bright, eager, hardworking college kid like me, but he had to go ahead and ask it anyway.

"You've actually hired people who *slept on the job*?" I replied, incredulous that anyone would dare.

He sighed and explained how, the summer before, they'd caught a few painters sleeping in the apartments that they were supposed to be painting.

We chuckled together for a few minutes at the absurdity of that, shaking our heads in disbelief.

Two months later, I was sleeping on the couch of an apartment I was supposed to be painting when the manager's secretary walked in.

"What's wrong with her?" she asked Joe, one of the painters rolling the living room walls.

"She said she wasn't feeling too well," Joe told her without skipping a beat. He was right, I *did* have a bad headache, but only because I'd been sleeping in the bedroom I'd just painted. It was one hundred degrees outside, so the windows in the apartment were all closed and the air-conditioning was on, recirculating paint fumes through the vents. We weren't very smart kids, though, or we'd probably be working in an office somewhere, making twice as much money for half the work.

Instead, we woke up at five-thirty every morning to paint the university's on-campus apartments all summer. During the first few weeks, we worked fast, conquering two or three apartments a day. Soon we were outpacing the spackling and repair teams that went into the unoccupied apartments ahead of us. Our supervisor, James, a big, easygoing guy, warned us that they were running out of stuff for us to paint.

"Y'all too fast," he told us, flat out. "Y'all gone run out of work if you keep this up."

And then, when the situation became dire, he got more ex-plicit: "Y'all only got *one more apartment* left after this, so . . . *take ya time.*"

So we came up with a new system to make our work stretch a little longer, hoping to stay employed through the end of the summer. We'd make sure to paint only one apartment each day. In order to do this, we'd split up the apartment into sections each morning, and each person could finish his or her section at any time during the day. Joe and Chip always took a nap immedi-ately, then finished the kitchen and the living room right before the end of the day. But Maggie and I liked to get our work out of the way first, so we'd each take a bedroom and paint it in the morning. I'd tape the room, cut in with a paintbrush, then roll the whole room twice in about three hours. After that, I'd close the door and take a nap on the mattress in the middle of the room, sucking in paint fumes as I slept.

After a few weeks of this, I finally concluded that it wasn't the air-conditioning but *the paint fumes* that were causing me to wake up with terrible headaches.

Although these toxic naps may have shaved years off my life, they never seemed all that risky as far as management finding out was concerned. No one from the main office aside from James ever stopped by the apartments where we were "working." Besides, they *had* to notice that we'd gone from painting two or three apartments a day to just one. Obviously we weren't work-ing at peak efficiency. Nobody seemed to mind. That is, until the day I was caught sleeping.

The whole thing made me feel like the worst sort of delin-quent. I hated the thought of the secretary going back to the office and telling the manager. They'd probably call me into the office and make me confess! What could I possibly say? I couldn't sit there and pretend that I was alone in my crime, that I blithely slept on the job while everyone else worked. What if they told potential future employers? But if I told the truth, why, I'd blow the lid off our whole operation! I'd jeopardize not just my job but everyone else's jobs, too! I imagined a dramatic scene like something out of *Law & Order*. I didn't want to screw up everyone else's situation but . . . no way could I go in there and lie right to their faces, either!

I sat there on the couch in the apartment, my mind reeling. There was no way out! So I did what any cornered professional does in a lose-lose situation: I got up from the couch, crept out the front door, practically tiptoed behind the main office, and walked all the way home, about two miles, in the hundred-degree heat, never to return again.

I probably overreacted. But then, bad jobs will compromise your ability to think straight, to reason, to draw logical conclusions from the information you're given. Bad jobs will show you sides of yourself you hardly recognize. Bad jobs will put you in situations you never imagined were possible.

The day after I walked home, Joe called me. "They say you can come back to work. They're not mad or anything. They'll probably just make you meet with the boss, and he'll tell you not to nap anymore, and that'll be it."

I got it. All I had to do was show up with a smile on my face, look busy, avoid making any unnecessary waves, and duck out the second my shift was over. But then I thought of that same manager, the one I had chuckled along with, shaking his head at me, and it made me sick to my stomach.

"That's okay," I told him. "I'll figure something else out."

SADLY, WHEN I GRADUATED from college, I discovered that professional jobs were just as bad as menial jobs, except you had to shower every morning and there weren't as many Lances around to openly despise your coworkers with you. Furthermore, not only were you expected to discuss the trivialities of your job in a tone of unflagging enthusiasm, you had to maintain this chipper tone in letters and e-mail correspondences and endless meetings, meetings that sprang up like stubborn weeds and prevented you from accomplishing any real work at all. In white-collar settings, the second you dropped the superhumanly positive tone, there were personality clashes and e-mail-based skirmishes in which you and some other sulky coworker tried to hurt each other using words, and before you knew it, you were out of a job and you had to start kissing ass and whistling Dixie all over again.

It wasn't about the work. Your quality and efficiency as a worker were beside the point. Intelligence and independent thought and creativity weren't just undervalued, they were a liability.

For some reason, it took me years to accept this. I would dodge meetings, refusing to admit that showing up and appearing engaged and helpful were the most important ways to keep my job. One well-timed, cheerful comment and I could safely while away the rest of the afternoon playing Tetris on my computer. Instead, I balked at how slowly and inefficiently my colleagues worked, not knowing that this was the *side work* of most jobs. The main requirement of any job was to be on time with a smile on your face, fire off a few chirpy e-mails, and go home. *Wet that bitch down and call it a night.*

My office jobs made me long for the relative satisfaction of *real work*—you know, digging ditches or flipping burgers or pulling weeds out of a gulley or breaking up rocks in the yard. Anything would be better than the existential oppression of fluorescent lighting and gray felt cubicle walls and the guy with the desk next to mine who answered the phone with the same phony "Hi, how ARE ya?" tone and cadence, hour after hour, day after day, world without end, Amen.

After a few years working at so-called respectable jobs, Lance's hopes and dreams made much more sense to me. Instead of striving to smile and chuckle and *Hi, how ARE ya?* his way to his next promotion, to a bigger office, to more responsibility, to more creative freedom, all of which are illusory sources of happiness anyway, as evidenced by the haggard, harried, palpably defeated middle managers and executives haunting the streets of our cities, Lance had created a carrot to dangle over his own head indefinitely. He was meant for greater things. He had talents that most people didn't know about. He believed in his big dreams, but he didn't need to achieve them to feel proud of himself. Whatever job he had would always be inconsequential, a tiny little fly in the big, rapidly melting ice cream sundae of life.

A FEW DAYS after I failed to detain that shoplifter, my future at the Gap ended abruptly. I was ready for my shift that afternoon, but my mom, who was supposed to drive me, never came home, and I couldn't reach her at work. After leaving several desperate messages on her voice mail, I called to warn Olivia that I'd probably be late.

"That is completely unacceptable," she growled. "When will you be here?"

"I don't know!" I was starting to panic in earnest. "My mom's not at her office. I don't know where she is!"

"Well, you'd better find some way to get here soon," she snapped, then hung up.

A half-hour later, my mom's car pulled into the driveway and I ran out to greet her in a state of panic. "Where have you been?! I *told* you I had to work today!"

"What? No you didn't!"

After we'd bickered for several minutes over who'd forgotten what, my mom finally said, "Well, either way, we'd better get going." At which point I burst into tears. "I can't go back there! *Don't make me go back!* I hate that woman! She's *crazy!*"

Then I explained about being put in charge of security and that tattling wimp Carol, and mean, nasty Olivia, who obviously hated my guts. What was her *problem*? It wasn't *my fault* that I didn't have a two-year-old with a no-account, rolling stone of a dad who laid his hat wherever the hell he felt like it!

My mom got quiet. She hated the mall and would sooner scrub toilets for a living than work there. And even though she came from the Tough Shit School of Parenting in most matters, she had a soft spot when it came to bad jobs. It wasn't the work, of course, but the crap you had to put up with from your coworkers.

"If you're really so unhappy, you should just call and quit. No job should make you that miserable."

"But I *can't* call and quit! I can't talk to that woman *ever again!*" This had to be handled with just the right touch, something that appealed to my mother's sense of justice. "She's not going to listen to me anyway! She's just going to lecture me about Gap protocol!"

My mom sighed. "Do you want me to call for you?"

"Do you mind?" I whimpered. I had her just where I wanted her.

"What do I care?" My mom picked up the phone, clearly stealing herself against whatever unknown flavor of unpleasantness was to come. "Hello, Olivia? This is Heather's mom. Yes. Well, there's been a misunderstanding. . . . Yes, I'm sure it is." Pause. "Well, Heather has decided that she's not going to come in. . . . Yes, she expected that." Long pause. "I see. Mmmhmm." Lots of talking on the other end. My mom's face was a blank. "Mmmhmm." Her tone was flat. "I see. Okay, okay. Good-bye, then." She put down the phone. "Jesus. I wouldn't want to work for that woman either."

There should probably be some dark moral to this story, something about the perils of skirting your responsibilities in the workplace. Maybe my experiences with Olivia could've taught me how crucial it is to communicate clearly and effectively with my colleagues, despite our differences. Perhaps I could've decided it was important to face down challenging situations by myself, like an *adult*, no matter how tough the circumstances.

Instead, I decided that I had the very best mommy in the whole wide world.

I was just like Lance, even then. I was determined to separate myself from the world of real work, to turn my back on other people's ideas of success, to thrive in my own little bubble. Even though I saw Lance's dreams as deluded, I quietly embraced my own delusions. Even as I scoffed at Olivia's superiority complex, I nursed my own feelings of superiority. But how else could we get by? People might chuckle at my sappy love songs or Lance's fashion designs, but they only laughed because they were anxious about their own secret dreams. Whether these things bring us success or recognition or not hardly matters. Anything that has the power to make the world seem big and full of promise is worth the effort.

And success doesn't fix everything. No one really arrives at some glorious end point. Life doesn't become relaxing and shiny and perfect one day, and all you have to do is wake up and eat cheese danishes by the pool. No matter how rich and famous and brilliant you are, you still have to tolerate inconvenient errands and lonely days and people who are so full of shit you can smell it on their breath through the telephone. You still have to tolerate unfolded sweaters and flies in your sundae.

Work can't just be a means to an end. You have to enjoy the means more than you fixate on the end. If your job is just a route to some sparkling future, the toad *work* will squat, and squat hard.

THIS MORNING I woke up early. The dogs and the children were still sleeping. I swept the floor in the kitchen, made some coffee, then settled into my chair by the window with my laptop in my lap. The cursor blinked on my screen, and for a moment I felt anxious. Was I fooling myself? Was I a dreamer? Would I still have a job next week?

A cool breeze floated in the window. It didn't really matter either way. I was ready to get to work.

11

A Tree Falls in the Forest

The morning after I lost my virginity, I woke up with a hangover at my friend Ann's house. I studied my glazed eyes in the bathroom mirror, splashed cold water on my face, and blotted it dry with a hand towel, then asked Ann to give me a ride to the ice cream shop where I worked. She dropped me off in front, I waved to the manager as I walked in, tied on my blue apron, and began removing lids from the ice cream bins in the freezer.

When it was time for my lunch break, I pulled the blue apron over my head, brushed the chocolate sprinkles off my clothes, and walked out of the air-conditioned chill of the store into the wet heat of the North Carolina summer. I crossed the four-lane road that separated the strip mall from its mothership, an enormous shopping mall. I exerted what felt like an unbearable effort just to hurry out of the way of approaching cars, my eyes squinting in the furious glare of the noontime sun. I walked across a sea of white, sparkling concrete, into the shade of the parking structure, through the doors at one end of the mall. I walked past

Belk's, past the Mantrap Hair Salon, up a flight of stairs, past the clothing boutique for big women, past the GTE store with the Mickey Mouse phone smiling in the window, to the Back Country store that sold preppy apparel to people who fancied themselves as rugged and outdoorsy. I stepped onto the echoing hardwood floor of the store, designed to look rustic under the neatly folded stacks of khakis in earthen hues and plaid button-up mountaineer shirts and old-fashioned long underwear with the square ass-flap in the back. I kept my eyes focused on the back wall of the store, walking past the perky girl who asked, "Can I help you?" like I was an actual consumer and not a fellow retail minion on a mission. I ignored her and walked to the back of the store, where I found him.

He looked big and scared. He was dressed like a lumberjack, in a plaid shirt with jeans and enormous tan work boots, a costume designed to imply that he might just toss a few sleeping bags and a tent into the back of his truck at any minute and head out to the mountains for a weekend of fishing. He was only eighteen, but he looked like a bright-eyed, fresh-faced, miniature version of Paul Bunyan.

"Hey. What's up?" he mumbled, doing his best to appear undaunted, but his eyes were round and frightened. His lumberjack boots shuffled nervously on the floorboards.

"Hey. Look. Last night was . . . no big deal. So don't worry about it," I told him.

"Oh . . . okay. That's cool."

"Just do me a favor?"

"Yeah?"

"Don't tell anyone about it."

"Okay, yeah! No problem."

"It's completely fine, but I *really* don't want you to tell anyone. Okay?"

"Yeah, no, that's—totally. Totally."

"Good. Okay. Well, see you later." I smiled and turned to leave. He seemed relieved. He was smiling, too. Was he glad I stopped by? Did that mean he liked me? Suddenly I had to rearrange all of the careful equations in my mind; suddenly my emergency plan seemed a little foolish. Maybe I should've just waited for him to call?

I walked a little slower, now, past the circular racks filled with navy sweatpants.

"Hey, hey, wait . . ."

I turned—he looked a little bashful, hopeful, even. No way—was he going to ask me out? He looked pretty good in his plaid shirt, there was no denying it. He had a big upper body that made him stand out among the skinny-shouldered boys of high school like a bull wandering among a pasture of wobbly-legged calves at a cattle ranch. Maybe he wanted to thank me, for fooling around with him in a drunken fog and then being really *understanding* and *practical* about it afterward, the most easygoing cow on the ranch, letting him know that I wasn't heartbroken or anything, that I wasn't reading into it and I wasn't about to call him or expect anything, letting him know that I *knew* that it was no big thing. He probably wanted to express his gratitude, to thank me for being so unbelievably cool, cool enough that he could almost consider the notion that we might be perfect for each other. . . .

"Um, I hope this isn't a problem, but . . . I sort of like your friend Ann."

Something inside me exploded. I struggled to muster a smile. "That's fine!" God, I was good at this, making my voice as bright and empty as possible. I was a natural-born fake.

"Really?"

"Yeah!" Laughter. Ha ha! Why would I care? "Of course. No worries."

"Cool, great!" he said, looking so relieved that I had a sudden urge to choke the life out of his empty face with my bare hands.

Instead I chuckled breezily and turned, walking past the stupid fucking kaleidoscope of plaid shirts and the moronic fucking red long underwear with that demeaning fucking butt-flap that no self-respecting human being could possibly consider wearing, not even a bona fide outdoorsman, as if such rugged types even came near a big, stupid mall like this one. I walked past the idiotic fucking ninety-dollar double-ply wool sweaters that no one would have any fucking *cause* to wear in North Carolina, not even in the dead of winter, and even if they did, they'd still have to take the stupid thing off the second they walked indoors because every indoor space in the entire fucking state was always heated to the boiling point all winter, forget that it was hardly even *freezing* outside, forget that climate control shouldn't mean climate *domination*, forcing everyone to wear short sleeves in every single indoor space anywhere, houses and schools included, forcing anyone who dared to dress practically to sweat profusely every time they walked inside.

But *everyone* was stupid. Everyone made crappy decisions,

everywhere you went. The world was filled with idiots, and I was the laughingstock of them all. To think of all the dumb people who would be getting a hearty laugh out of me, in my stupidity, my pathetic-slut maneuvering, sleeping with someone just because I was anxious to get it over with, make it happen, casting the white candles and true love aside for a pathetic romp in my friend's little sister's bed, for no reason at all. Even Ann, who didn't have any way of knowing what happened, would eventually find out and she and her new lumberjack boyfriend would get a good laugh about it and she'd tell everyone and they'd all laugh together at what a pathetic slutty loser I was. And of course *I* was the one who would look really sad in that picture, not him. He got lucky, what's wrong with that? He was eighteen and horny. *He was just doing his job.*

Back in the chill of the ice cream store, with my blue apron on again, I soothed the pounding in my head and the beery paste on my tongue and the dull ache of shame that saturated my limbs by crafting a careful philosophy to frame the whole ugly mess, to get my thoughts and feelings under control. I needed to put it all in perspective. I needed to pack it up in a box and hide it away once and for all: *This is not a tragedy,* I told myself. *This isn't tragic.* Losing your virginity to an oaf when you're drunk and then finding out that he likes one of your best friends isn't *really* all that sad, not really, even if it seems sad from the outside. It certainly doesn't doom you to be a reject forever, it doesn't even *matter,* it's no big deal. This is the kind of thing that's blown up as important by other people, stupid people who romanticize sex for no good reason, who treat virginity like it's a big deal just to keep girls from sleeping around, when, really, it's not all that important, it's just something dumb that happened . . . *as long as no one ever finds out about it.* As long as no one knows about it—and he *just said* he wouldn't tell anyone, didn't he? And *you're* certainly not going to tell anyone—then *it's just like it never happened.*

If a tree falls in the forest, but no one is there to hear it, does it make a sound? No, I decided. It makes no sound at all.

AND SO THE WORLD went on soundlessly spinning that day, and even though I tried to tell myself that it didn't matter, I still felt toxic and dehydrated and ashamed. I'd made a move on someone who clearly didn't like me, and then I hadn't even managed to *stop it* from going too far. I was intrigued by how far he was willing to push it, in the house of this girl whom he now said he "liked," to push it without any signs or feedback from me. I was amazed by his audacity, by his fumbling insistence. And it was easier to watch it all happen, to do nothing. Could it just happen, without any input from me at all?

Years of passive fantasies of the good girl had led me to this sordid fate. Good girls weren't aggressors, after all. You didn't fantasize about actively ravishing someone. No way. Some dirty guy has his way with you while you mildly protested. Bad man! Filthy, sweaty, panting, burly stud! Your virginity was something intangible that a pushy guy would eventually steal away with, and he would prize it far more than you ever did. You didn't even know what it was, couldn't see it, couldn't feel it. It was there for the taking.

Even so, I was a little disappointed. I'd barely felt a thing, and it was over so quickly. I'd had make-out sessions that were more intense. And even though I'd never completely bought into the hazy dream world presented by movies like *Endless Love*—where beautiful teenage girls and beautiful teenage boys lit millions of little white candles, stared into each other's eyes, expressed their undying love for each other, then got naked— now that it was over, I couldn't quite believe that I'd wasted my big moment on an apathetic stranger. I could've slept with Andy O'Brien, the shy soccer player I'd dated that spring who bought me sixteen long-stemmed red roses for my sixteenth birthday. He would've gone in for the whole millions-of-little-white-candles thing—hell, he would've happily lit them all himself while I sipped red wine and watched. But he was pale and nervous and he always had this strange, sharp stubble above his lip so that every time he kissed me it felt like he was trying to scratch off my lips with sandpaper.

But I couldn't get all romantic about the first time *now*. Jesus. Just because the whole world ascribed virtue to staying pure and innocent for as long as possible, that didn't mean I believed it. Years of Catholicism had taught me to hold such notions in disdain, to see them as just another trick to keep your panties on, to lead you not unto temptation but deliver you from evil. Wasn't I above all of that narrow-minded nonsense? Wasn't I happy to deliver myself straight into the hands of evil, and to breezily tell evil that everything was cool, I could hang with whatever, I was fine, I didn't mind? No problem, no worries.

As long as no one knew. It would be bad if someone knew. If someone knew, then *everyone* would know. They'd all know and they'd think that I was a sad little slut.

Half of the girls at my high school had had sex long before that summer, the summer before my junior year, and by the end of the year the lumberjack, with his square shoulders and big arms, became known for pushing a wide assortment of virgins into sleeping with him. Some girl lost it in the bathroom of her house during a party while her parents were out of town. Another girl lost it in the backseat of someone else's car. Hearing about those girls didn't help. Were they tricked? Did they like him? It didn't matter. Somehow they still couldn't have been as pathetic as I was. *They* were just having fun.

My friend Ann, to her credit, dumped the lumberjack after a few weeks, concluding that he was dumb, shallow, not that sexy, had bad taste in music, and had a very, very small penis. I hadn't noticed and had no real point of comparison, but in retrospect his small size was probably the one merciful gift from the gods in the whole sordid picture. And maybe it explained his behavior just a little. To navigate high school with a big lumberjack body and a tiny little axe to grind: He had to feel like something of a false advertisement, under the circumstances. Although in high school, surrounded by inexperienced girls like me, it wasn't much of a liability, practically speaking. Based on what I'd read and seen on TV, it would eventually be an embarrassment for him, though. I should probably pity him. He did seem pretty hapless. In truth, I never really blamed him for anything. I just tried to put him out of my mind.

There were *real* catastrophes that took place over the years that followed, catastrophes that completely dwarfed my private melodrama. There was the sixteen-year-old girl who drove her brand-new bright red car off the road at seventy miles an hour on the way to a party, hit a mound of dirt, fell out of the car, and died on the spot. There was my gay friend who was a Jehovah's Witness, who couldn't talk to his parents, and who didn't even know why he was friends mostly with girls and had crushes on all the guys he knew. There was the cheerleader whose mom had hung herself in their basement. The girl showed up at school a few days later as smiley and bubbly as ever, as though nothing had happened, and we, stupidly, marveled at how *well* she was handling the whole thing.

But this little part of my history still felt tragic, somehow. I couldn't reinvent the world and place myself in the middle of a different reality. It was 1987, North Carolina, and I was technically a slut for this one little indiscretion, this one tiny moment of bad judgment. But only *I* knew it, I reminded myself over and over. The lumberjack himself probably didn't even remember, I was one of so many.

At least no one knows. Thank God no one knows.

ELEVEN YEARS LATER at my ten-year high school reunion, I was talking with an old friend about all of the ridiculous, embarrassing stuff that we went through way back when, and she mentioned in passing, casually, that I'd lost my virginity to the lumberjack.

"What?" I mumbled, dumbfounded. "How did you know about that?"

She said, laughingly, that everyone knew about it. The lumberjack had told everyone, *every single person he could tell*, and they told everyone *they* could tell. *Everyone* knew.

Did anyone *not* know? No, it was common knowledge, just like all of the other girls I'd known that he'd had sex with. I was a part of that lore the whole time, the whole time I was working so hard to tell myself it wasn't tragic, it wasn't sad, it wasn't anything I didn't want it to be. I didn't control this picture.

I REMEMBER SEEING the lumberjack on the couch in Ann's house, after everyone else had gone to sleep. He was too drunk to drive home, and all of our friends were already staying over. Ann had gone upstairs to sleep in her parents' bed like a smart girl—she didn't really know him, after all.

I think I knew that he liked Ann. It wasn't like he'd given me any indication that he liked *me*. This was the torture of having beautiful friends—not just cute girls, but truly beautiful girls, tall and slim and well put together and confident. I was the comic relief. I could talk, sure, and sing and dance and make everyone laugh. I charmed the strangers, I kept everyone smiling. I wasn't bad-looking, not bad at all. But I knew I was never the one the *really* cute guys wanted. Guys would swoon over Ann, they'd act like they were far more sophisticated and sensitive than they actually were, just to be around her.

I knew that I would get the sidekick, the other guy, the less interesting, less confident, less funny one. He'd look at me and I'd look at him and we'd both grimace and think, "Leftovers." We'd make out, sure, whatever, but I knew that he liked Ann the best, and he knew that I liked his taller, cuter friend.

So I got grabby. I saw the lumberjack on the couch. I wanted something exciting to happen to *me*. This was how I got when I drank: The world seemed to expand and become full of endless possibilities, and then everyone went to bed alone, and I was never ready for that abrupt ending. The alcohol in my veins insisted that big things could happen, big things *should* happen, the world was filled with promise and I was beautiful, just as beautiful as any of the others, just as mesmerizing. I was dressed in white, I was flanked by roses and candles. Part of me thought that if he took a close look at me, if we talked for a second, he would notice that I was much prettier than he thought, plus I was the soundtrack, I was the charming one. So I walked in and sat down, but we barely talked, we just made out.

No self-respecting girl behaved that way, I knew that, but some part of me imagined that just by kissing him, he would wake up and realize that I was the one who was worth his time. I knew Ann was only mildly interested. I knew she was on the fence. I was the one who really needed this. She would see that clearly, soon enough.

Now I think that I probably deserved it, the shame of it all. To disregard Ann's feelings, to grab before her story could unfold. I deserved the Frogger walk of shame, dodging cars in the sweltering heat on my way to the mall. I deserved to be told what I already knew, deep inside: I wasn't his first pick, and no amount of beery, reckless abandon would change my fate.

What I didn't know was that Ann never trusted me again, and then, a few months later, she stole the guy I liked, who liked me, too, and I thought it was merely an act of selfishness, not an act of revenge. And I suppose it could all be chalked up to the foolishness of high school girls, the same old stuff that happens year after year, all over the place. But I didn't have female friends for years after that; I imagined that they were all untrustworthy. Somehow I never looked at myself and asked if *I* was worthy of trust. I knew myself too well—my hurts and my vulnerabilities and my fears. I knew how damaged and scared I felt, how each rejection piled up, quietly, and never got thrown out. I thought my friends didn't feel these things. When they said they did, I thought they were exaggerating. I thought they were immune. I thought they had an easier path, paved by their looks and their money and their tendency to speak in blustery, overconfident terms. I used the same practiced, confident tone myself, but I figured that my friends could see right through it, to my fragile, shaking heart.

I never meant to hurt Ann, but how could someone like her be hurt by *me,* anyway? She'd laugh it off. She was impervious. She'd see that these things didn't come to me like they did to other girls. She'd generously let me take what I could get, because she knew she had a gaggle of guys ready to drool and swoon and hang on her every word waiting for her, just around the next corner.

We could've talked it through, of course, but that meant admitting what I had done, admitting that I'd gotten grabby, that I wasn't the only one with feelings in the picture. I was too ashamed of the whole thing, and it was far better to *seem*— to seem confident and happy and undaunted. Otherwise, why would anyone want to be my friend? Otherwise, how could I ever be anyone's first pick?

But I was all alone in my revised narrative, in my climate-controlled emotional state. My friendship with Ann crumbled, and nothing added up, nothing made any sense. I felt misunderstood without being remotely open to the fact that other people felt sad and small, too. I had been defeated but I wouldn't admit it. I stopped letting people in, and then, eventually, I wondered where all my friends went.

If a tree falls in the forest, even if it looks like no one is there to hear it, they're there. And they're listening.

SOMETIMES I FLY over the old ice cream store and the mall and Ann's house in my mind, and I think about how scared and lonely we all were, hiding from each other in plain sight. I imagine all of the girls who lost their virginity in bathrooms and in the backs of cars, picturing them married with kids, or living in the city and walking to work in tall shoes on a blustering fall day. Strangely, I feel the most sorry for the lumberjack. He was needier than any of us, somehow, even if it wasn't something that anyone, not even he, could see clearly back then.

Ann and I were sitting around my house in Los Angeles one afternoon this fall, talking about my daughter's second-birthday party and Ann's latest date with a songwriter. We tell each other the truth now, at all costs, even when it makes us feel ashamed in retrospect, to know that there's a person out there who knows our flaws, our worries, our regrets, our mistakes. The truth is only possible when you don't worry about sounding pathetic, when you can admit that other people might know better than you, that they might see how flawed you are, that they might clearly recognize your missteps and maybe even laugh at them and feel smug to know that they'd never make the same bad decisions themselves.

Sometimes, because of our long history, it's easier to tell Ann the truth than anyone else. Sometimes, because of our long history, it's harder to tell her. Occasionally, I'm ashamed to think of all she knows. Sometimes when I talk to her, I still feel like the sidekick, the also-ran, the ugly duckling, the grabby slut, the loser, and it makes me angry to think that she doesn't quite recognize that I'm *none* of those things anymore. I'm different, I'm strong, I get it now, I'm in control.

But I'm not in control, not really. The sidekick, the also-ran, the ugly duckling, the grabby slut, they're still a part of me. They fuel something unpredictable and sad in me, something that drives me forward. They color my perspective. They feed my anger and my gratitude. They put me in my place but also offer me jokes and opinions and insights, and if I kicked them to the curb for good, I'd be alone again, in a climate-controlled hell of disconnection, of empty, anxious striving, fixated on perfection.

I can't completely lose that hungover, glazed-eyed girl in the blue apron, the one with the much cuter friend, the one with the sweaty palms and the foggy head as she marches into the mall. But she knows that red pajamas and wool sweaters are preposterous. She knows that most teenage boys don't care about the candles and the roses, not really.

She's okay by me. But I don't care anymore for that imagined self I presented back then and in those lonely years that followed, that swaggering, lovable nothing, that bawdy fun-time girl, cool with everything, no problems and no worries, spilling over with false confidence.

If a tree falls in the forest, it makes a thundering boom. And then it's over, and it's quiet again, and the whole thing really isn't as bad as you imagined it would be. You dust yourself off and keep walking, across the mossy forest floor, through the dappled sunlight.

12

Tell Me the Truth

As soon as I moved to San Francisco, my dad started making plans for the two of us to go wine tasting together. He didn't tell me that I was the designated driver until we rolled into Napa. "In the old days, *everyone* on the road was wasted," he explained with the fond tone of someone describing a simpler, better time. "But now there are cops all over the place, so *watch your back!*"

My job was to take the occasional sip but stay sober, a real challenge for a twenty-four-year-old lush. My dad's job was to get drunk on free wine, harass any wine pourers or tasters who appeared to take their bourgeois pastime a little too seriously, and flirt with all attractive, youngish women within spitting distance. Oh, and to never, ever spit. Spitting was for lightweights.

This was how he ended up making boozy friends with Doug and Jen, the sort of preppy young couple for whom wine tasting in Napa is a relationship rite of passage. Jen was a compact blonde with an immediate wine-addled grin for my dad, welcoming his vaguely dismissive flavor of flirtation with the open wonderment of someone who'd been mistaking condescension for genuine interest since her sorority days; Doug was a blank slate of easy-going passivity belted up in golf shorts and a lime-green polo shirt. He seemed to while away the afternoon in a distracted haze, blurting, "I hear ya!" or "Right! Right!" occasionally, and then settling back into some barely conscious head-nodding state.

After the two of them had chuckled amiably down whatever half-insulting path my dad chose for almost an hour, we gathered up some bread and cheese and another bottle of wine and had lunch together under the shade of some low trees outside.

Halfway through lunch, Jen turned to me without warning and hissed, urgently, "How old do you think I am? *Guess!*"

I looked into her squinting eyes, with their faint crow's-feet. This felt like a trap.

"Guess! Just *guess!*" she slurred at my nose.

I studied her neck. "Thirty-five," I said.

"Oh my God! You're right," she gasped, disappointed. *"How can you tell?"*

"Mostly by that wrinkle across the middle of your neck," I said, cutting more cheese off a nearby hunk and smearing it on some bread. "Only women who lie out in the sun too much get that in their twenties. Otherwise it shows up later." Jen reflexively grabbed at her neck, horrified.

It really didn't occur to me how terrible that would sound to her, coming from a woman ten years younger. I had no idea that the stakes to this guessing game were higher than I could possibly imagine, that the rule of thumb with any woman over twenty-eight was to err on the young side, then subtract four, or that no matter how accurate your guess turned out to be, you should never, *ever*, mention any empirical evidence you'd gathered to support your hypothesis.

The wheels seemed to come off Jen's happy buzz-wagon after that, and she and Doug soon excused themselves and retreated back to their hotel, where a long nap and the solace of their mutual resignation awaited them.

That afternoon, I realized that even when people look you right in the eye and urge you to tell them the truth, that doesn't mean they really want it. The truth rarely sets you free. In most cases, the truth sends you to the nearest bed with a sharp headache and a sudden urge to puke your guts out.

BUT I SHOULD'VE KNOWN that already, since my mom had a habit of asking for the truth and then regretting it later. I was only thirteen when she announced to me and my sister in the car—lightly, casually—that *the second* we started having sex, we should come to her and tell her about it so that she could get us on the pill. She made the whole thing sound like something fun and breezy she'd help us with, like calling to order a pizza on a whim. We'd go on the pill, and that way we wouldn't get pregnant. Simple!

We both groaned so she'd understand that *that was disgusting*. Obviously neither one of us would ever be having sex.

Well, she knew we wouldn't be having sex anytime soon, but when we were ready, the *very first thing* we should do was come to her and tell her about it. It was important. She wouldn't judge, no way! She would be thrilled to help us be responsible about it.

Four years later when I started sleeping with my boyfriend, I told my mom immediately.

"Oh, God! Why are you telling me this?" she moaned, barely able to look me in the eye.

"Because I thought you would want to know!"

"I wish you hadn't told me."

"But you told me to tell you when I started having sex!"

"I did? Jesus. Why did I say that?"

"You said I should tell you so I could see a doctor and go on the pill!"

"The pill! Oh my God." She covered her eyes, obviously wishing I would disappear.

My mom's lofty goals sometimes exceeded her emotional capacity. She sincerely wanted to be the welcoming, easygoing, modern mom, but taking her invitations to speak frankly meant waking up in an emotional fun house, with mazes of mirrors and floors that tilted under your feet. At the very moment when I'd been assured I'd be guided by the *I'm OK—You're OK* hippie mom of my dreams, my fearless, open-minded mother assumed the fetal position. Like Jen in her hotel bathroom, furiously rubbing expensive moisturizer into the wrinkle on her neck, my mom couldn't handle the truth.

Naturally, I took this as an invitation to lie with impunity.

BUT EVEN AS I LEARNED to lie whenever it was mildly convenient to do so, I couldn't accept the idea that anyone would ever lie to me. My lies were irrelevant or circumstantial; other people's lies were a clear indication of some essential flaw in their character, a reflection on their lack of integrity as human beings.

During the fall of my junior year in high school, I fell asleep every single afternoon in French class. It was right after lunch, and the classroom was always so warm that I couldn't keep my eyes open. *Je ne peux pas parce que les deux yeux ne . . .* Those droning French words ran together in a muddle of white noise, the perfect sonic pillow on which to rest my tired head.

I wasn't the only one. Halfway through the year, our teacher, Madame Barber, announced that she'd be handing out "Bon Points" as an incentive for answering her queries in class. Each time we spoke, we'd get a little piece of paper with the words "1 Bon Point" written on it. At the end of the year, the student with the most Bon Points would get five points added to his or her final grade.

My friend Amy raised her hand and asked a question in halting French, then studied the small rectangular piece of paper Madame Barber handed her.

"We can just Xerox these things!" she whispered to me, grinning.

We chortled behind our hands at how easy it would be to fix the Bon Point game, but I forgot about it until the end of the year, when Madame Barber told us all to count up our Bon Points for her.

I had seventy-four filthy, crumpled Bon Points, which seemed like a lot. I'd resorted to drinking two Cokes at lunch just to keep my eyes open, and ended up prattling on in French in a caffeine-addled state.

I glanced over at Amy, who fumbled in her purse for a few minutes, then counted out a remarkably fat, crisp-looking stash of Bon Points. "One hundred and four!" she announced triumphantly. Madame Barber was very impressed, and retrieved Amy's Bon Points with a congratulatory nod of respect while the rest of us rolled our eyes.

"*Did you photocopy Bon Points?*" I whispered a few minutes later, when no one was paying attention.

"No!" Amy replied. "I've been talking a lot lately. Haven't you noticed?"

I figured she didn't want to admit the truth in class, in case someone was listening, so afterward in the hallway I asked her again. "You photocopied those, right?" It wasn't like I was going to tell on her or anything, I just wanted to know.

"No, I swear, I really didn't," she said, eyes wide like she meant it this time. "I talk all the time in there."

"You can tell me, I won't be mad," I said, even though I was a little annoyed that she would put the Bon Points plan into motion without telling me. "It's no big deal."

"Oh, believe me, I considered it, but I decided not to because I had so many anyway." Amy was a pretty good liar, I knew that. I'd seen her twist the truth to suit her needs before. She always sounded so casually convincing when she did it, so matter-of-fact and relaxed. But why would she lie to *me*? We knew everything about each other. We told each other everything. Could she be telling the truth?

Two weeks later, I was hanging out in Amy's living room, waiting for her to get back from the bathroom and there, among the books and videotapes on the coffee table, was a photocopied page of a scattered pile of Bon Points.

I didn't say anything to Amy, I just picked up the page, folded it, and slipped it into my pocket. I didn't want to confront her or embarrass her, really. But I needed to save the evidence, evidence that she was *a liar* and couldn't be trusted.

But who could afford to be honest, at our age? As a teenager, once you figured out that almost everyone—parents, teachers, friends, boyfriends—had no real use for the truth, what else could you do but lie? Everyone wanted a different version of you: a pure-hearted, virginal child who never wanted to grow up; a hardworking, dedicated student who lived to learn; a supportive, faithful listener who could empathize with anything; or a carefree gal who loved to make out but wasn't prone to crying jags. If you told the truth and admitted that you were selfish and lazy and slutty and neurotic and hopelessly insecure, it was pretty clear that no one would want anything to do with you. Lies were, at that age, a matter of survival. Kids who told the truth all the time were mediocre students with disappointed parents who had no friends, no boyfriend, and no fun whatsoever.

When I asked Amy about it years later, she said she'd photocopied the Bon Points but then felt guilty and decided not to use them. Even if she *had* used them, though, and had lied through her teeth when I grilled her about it, that wasn't such a departure from the inherent corruption of adolescence. I saved that page of Bon Points as proof that Amy wasn't trustworthy, when really, at most, it was only proof that Amy and I were a lot alike. Unscrupulous, maybe, but adaptive.

.   .   .

AFTER ABOUT FIFTEEN YEARS of lying through my teeth, I went into therapy and learned that I should tell the truth about everything. I was listening to a lot of Alanis Morissette at the time—embarrassing, sure, but I kept telling myself that *that was the whole point*—songs about being honest about what a mess you are, songs about kicking bad habits and thanking entire continents and the universe itself for making you just the way you are. As good as it felt to slough off over a decade of defense mechanisms and protective camouflage, to walk through the world as naked and vulnerable and open as a child (the kind of child I'd been snickering at for the previous fifteen years), I was a little worried that I'd lose my edge in the process. Without a constant flow of lies—lies about how confident I was, lies about knowing everything about myself and my flaws before anyone else could open their mouths, lies about not wanting a boyfriend and not caring about what anyone thought, lies about sincerely enjoying that Ween concert two years ago—I would just be an ordinary person. Honesty and openness threatened to make me as dull and uncritical as the other honest, open people I knew—although, granted, there weren't that many of them.

My therapist, Alan, assured me that it wouldn't be like that at all, that I was on a search for my *authentic self*. Finding it sounded a little bit like being high all the time: I would breathe in the world with heightened senses. I would feel things more deeply. I would be filled with a strong sense of gratitude. Once my hard, cynical former self was burned away, I would emerge with a more genuine flavor of confidence, a far cry from the hollow swagger I'd adopted out of desperation, under the bewildering circumstances of my emotionally unpredictable household.

Alan was the sort of person who you could see had benefited from the regular, concentrated infusions of confidence that come from a rigorous daily schedule of self-esteem building. He was tall and lanky and had a certain flair for drama that you don't typically find in middle-aged shrinks. Alan was once an actor, before he became a Buddhist and a professional listener. He'd mentored under a guy who wrote books about the adult children of alcoholics, books filthy with acronyms to explain the most common dysfunctional behaviors—Blaming, Lies, Addiction, Defensiveness—spelling out words like SHAME and NUTJOB and INTOLERABLE CONTROL FREAK.

Alan had been schooled in the art of empathic attunement, which basically meant that he appeared to be incredibly moved by my hour-long monologues about the unspeakable pain of having my mother book my airline tickets to my cousin's wedding without consulting me first. I would walk into his office feeling slightly awkward, like he was a guy I'd slept with on a drunken binge but hardly remembered, and then minutes later I'd be sobbing into my hands about how no one really understood me and no one ever really tried, just like that Kate Bush song goes. But driving home from his office an hour later, I felt a sense of clarity, like my windshield had been cleaned for the first time in decades.

Nonetheless, there was something a little precious and rarefied about what we were doing, something I didn't completely trust. Walking into that room was an exercise in the suspension of disbelief. Like any good therapist, Alan pretended to care, while I pretended that I was a sweet, loving, pure-hearted soul being excavated from layers and layers of corrupting influences. The process itself felt corrupt, like an old guy paying for a lap dance from a hot young girl who wouldn't have so much as nodded at him on the street if there weren't money involved.

Besides, weren't the lies I'd chosen part of who I was, too? Sure, it made sense to dig for some innocent inner child to embrace, since my adult self had become too sullen and hungover and bitter to deserve a hug on any given day. I had to find some way to stop beating myself up over everything (even though I really did deserve to have my ass kicked). Therapy *was* working in many ways: I was starting to drop my defenses, starting to tell the truth more, and I felt pretty good—fragile, but *invigorated* by my newfound fragility. I could feel my emotions without beating them back or judging them badly—or at least I could try to, occasionally.

But was my personality as a child—honest, open, full of wonder, prone to weeping at the slightest provocation—somehow more *authentic* than the pessimistic, spiteful cad I'd become? Was it really fair to claim such innocence and purity as my true self, or to throw away years of meticulously constructed defense mechanisms, many of them awesomely complex and imaginatively designed, the psychological equivalent of the internal-combustion engine?

Maybe, instead, I was some unsteady combination of innocent (and occasionally sullen) child and cynical (and occasionally warm) adult. My genuine self was at once kind *and* nasty, well-intentioned *and* short-tempered *and* avoidant *and* thoughtful *and* hesitant to shower regularly.

And even though most people had seemed to want nothing but lies from me from the time I was little, could you really blame them? Open, innocent, honest little children can be seriously annoying, let's face it. If someone doesn't shame them out of that state when they're young, they grow up to be the sorts of impractical free-range idealists who vomit into their hands at the barbecue because someone forgot to warn them that the buns for the organic veggie hot dogs weren't entirely wheat-free.

I soon found that, like such exotic dietary requirements, the flavor of unconditional positive regard that Alan had to offer wasn't exactly reproducible in the real world. I walked out of his office each week armed with the deluded notion that I could tell the truth— the whole truth and nothing but the truth—and the world would embrace me for it. Nothing could've been further from the truth. In fact, the only people who enjoy compulsively confessional women are free-range idealists, drug-addled hippies, and therapists in training—who are often, not surprisingly, INTOLERABLE CONTROL FREAKS.

Thus, two years after I started therapy, I dragged my intolerable-control-freak, therapist-in-training boyfriend to Alan's office so we could both (as long as we were being honest!) confess how intolerable we found each other. The control freak was once an actor, you see, but he was training to become a Buddhist and a professional listener, so he and Alan had a lot in common. Nonetheless, Alan didn't seem to like him very much (which I could completely understand and relate to).

Strangely enough, instead of pointing out the obvious fact that the intolerable control freak and I were both depressed and quite possibly hated each other's guts to boot, Alan encouraged us to continue "doing the work" of engaging in honest dialogue, most of it consisting of expressions of scorn and resentment couched in the thinnest veneer of civility. Ironically, what a couple like me and the control freak *really* needed to make our relationship last was to lie to each other around the clock.

So, in the interest of remaining committed to our ideals of commitment and embracing each other's inner children (who were serious brats), the intolerable control freak and I stayed together for two miserable years. Finally, when I was home for Christmas and experiencing a temporary bout of sanity (that I might've mistaken for cynicism were I in Alan's office), I dumped my boyfriend over the phone. He didn't sound upset at all, and quickly confessed that he was, quite frankly, relieved. How had we taken our shared interest in emotional truth and turned it into a gigantic, elaborate lie that made us both crazy . . . or, *crazier*, at any rate?

One year later, I returned to therapy with Alan, only to find that he had rented out an office in his suite to my ex. Alan was very apologetic about it, but when he was explaining himself, I noticed how incredibly *genuine* and *authentic* he sounded, hands folded, lips pursed intently. Suddenly I saw him for what he was: a very talented actor, one who was skillfully covering his tracks in the wake of a questionable judgment call. That sweetly sensitive tilt to his head, that thoughtful squint? He would truly *hate* for me to feel in the least bit uncomfortable about the fact that my former boyfriend (who had once given me a black eye, which I eventually forgave him for, thanks to lots of open, honest dialogue in that very office) now occupied the office *right down the hall* from him (but Alan was really so sorry about the whole thing, making it sound like the result of a lack of full disclosure on the part of my ex, albeit one that he, Alan, appeared unwilling or unable to address and/or remedy). If I felt *at all* uncomfortable, he would *truly* understand . . . and apparently do nothing about it whatsoever. See how open, honest talk helps so very, *very* much?

I lied and said it was no big deal, that I still spoke to the self-deluded motherfucker from time to time, and I wished that temperamental asshole nothing but the very best. At the end of our session, I wrote Alan a check, smiled warmly as I walked out the door, and never went back.

The inner child we discovered together might still be there, in Alan's office, weeping and snotting all over his couch. That's okay, Alan can look after her for me. She's probably better off there, where she can languish in the stagnancy of imaginary unconditional positive regard indefinitely. After all, Alan is far better at playing make-believe than I'll ever be.

"SHE REALLY HAS YOUR NUMBER, THAT ONE." My mother is pointing out that my two-year-old is the boss of me, something that I've known for quite some time. I try to draw lines in the sand, sure, but it's pure folly. My daughter is in control. I am her helpless little puppet.

Still, it's not entirely relaxing to find yourself—one month postpartum with your second child, crabby from getting about four hours of sleep a night, cowed by an increasingly bossy and somewhat shell-shocked two-year-old—fielding strongly worded advice from your mother about your child-rearing skills. I have tried to explain that Claire *just* started acting this way, all weird and petulant and demanding, and even though we know it's normal and we expected it, both my husband and I are still baffled every time she throws a fit. We might be armed with a plan—more time-outs! firm boundaries!—but that plan changes on the spot, as we wonder if more softness isn't warranted, given how Claire's world has been turned upside down so recently by her brand-new little sister.

My mom encounters these explanations with all the acceptance of an atheist at a Baptist revival. To her, my husband and I are suckers, living under the tiny thumb of a master manipulator.

But my mom only recently started acting this way, all weird and petulant and demanding. She just retired, one of her closest friends is very sick, and she's extremely grouchy about getting old herself. Instead of hiding behind passive-aggressive remarks like she has for most of her life, she's telling it like it is. She's finally become the fearless, straight-talking mom of my dreams—and it sucks.

So one day we're driving across town in my car and I can't take it anymore. I break down and tell her, *Look, you have to back off a little! I know you're only trying to help, but Bill and I don't need to hear how pathetic and powerless we are every time our merciless toddler queen enters the room! We have better things to do, like drop to our knees and genuflect, for one thing . . .*

"But you *told* me to tell you the truth!" my mom cries.

And she's right. I had urged her, practically begged her, to be frank with me. I had announced—lightly, casually—that *the second* she had something she needed to get off her chest, she should come to me and tell me about it so that I wouldn't have to guess what she was feeling when she quibbled about the real meaning of the verb "hedge" or the fact that the spaghetti was overcooked. I made the truth sound like something fun and breezy I'd help her with, like rearranging her furniture. We'd be honest with each other, and that way, we wouldn't misunderstand each other ever again. Simple!

But the truth was messy and harsh and it was coming out all over the place, all the time, in ways that I couldn't have anticipated. Sure, she'd start with a disclaimer, then she'd immediately knock it over like the straw man that it was.

"It's not like I'm sitting around judging you or the job you're doing as a parent . . ." she began after a particularly hectic morning together when the baby was crying incessantly, Bill and I were bickering over the contents of the diaper bag, and Queen Claire had decreed that pants would not be worn out the front door henceforth.

I breathed a sigh of relief. *She's not judging me at all, she understands,* I thought.

"I just worry about the state of your marriage," she added. Sweet Jesus.

"You really don't need to worry about our marriage," Bill interjected. "At least not my side of it. We're just not sleeping, and it's making us both crazy."

"Oh, believe me, I know that every couple has their little squabbles," my mom told him, and I could feel myself relax again. "But those little fights add up. And look, sometimes men don't realize how much that kind of bickering bothers them *until they're already out the door.*"

. . .

MY MOTHER, as it turns out, is just as negative as I'd always suspected her to be, back when, instead of stating her feelings directly, she'd furiously vacuum the rug, or point out rather vehemently that my porcelain candle holders looked like they'd break if you so much as *glanced* at them the wrong way. Now I sometimes find myself longing for those days when my mom spoke only in code.

Still, I try to breathe deeply and keep things upbeat. This isn't a terrible relationship like the one I had with my control-freak ex. I really *do* want to know what my mom is thinking or feeling, even if she's not all that gentle about it. Neither one of us is all that gentle when it comes to speaking honestly.

So in the car, when she reminds me that I asked her to tell the truth, I agree.

"You're right. I did say that. And I *do* want you to tell me the truth. I'm just not very good at hearing it yet."

"Well, me neither."

We keep driving for a few minutes in silence. Finally, I start thinking about how lucky I am. I have a fantastic husband, a generous, helpful mother who, when we're not arguing, has a great sense of humor and makes really good apple pie. And now I have not one but *two* daughters.

"I feel lucky that I have two daughters," I blurt to my mom, because that's just the sort of thing you can blurt to your mom, when you have an honest, open relationship with her like I do. "It suits me, really, to have two girls."

"And they'll break your heart," my mother mutters in a low voice.

"Jesus Christ, you are *dark*. I mean, you are really, *really* dark."

"That's not dark, it's a fact. They'll break your heart. That's how kids are. They never love you as much as you love them. How is that dark?"

"You know, as long as we're being honest? I think that you are fucking *insane*." I start to laugh. "Maybe that's just me, maybe I'm crazy, too. I probably am. But all I know for sure is that you are *certifiable*. You are totally, completely off your rocker."

"Well, no one thinks you're as crazy as your own kids do. But really, you're the only person I know who thinks so."

"Ha! Sorry, but I seriously doubt it. You should feel grateful that you have so many self-restrained friends."

"Maybe."

We drive in silence after that, my mom thinking I'm sort of a jerk, me thinking how lucky we are. We'll break each other's hearts, of course. And we'll still lie sometimes.

We are so lucky.

13

One Ring to Rule Them All

F ind someone early, don't wait!"

My father's thirtysomething girlfriend leaned across the table to deliver this advice in a stage whisper. I was only nineteen years old, and my father was within earshot. But Alice had tossed back a few glasses of red wine and she was winding up for one of her soliloquies. She didn't have kids (not that she didn't want them!) and she needed to save me from the same uncertain fate.

"Oh, really?" I stabbed my steak with my fork, hoping she'd see how little I felt like discussing this in front of my dad.

"Yes, really!" she said, sitting back in her chair. "I'm serious, Heather. When I think about the *great* guys I dated in college, guys who would've married me in a *heartbeat*? Jesus . . ." She trailed off, looking over at my noncommittal, three-girlfriend-minimum, fifty-year-old professor dad who was polishing off his halibut, hardly listening to her words.

I studied Alice across the table. What was wrong with her? She was reasonably attractive, smart, opinionated, and she seemed to like drinking. She was anything but boring. Maybe she was too demanding or too bossy and she went on and on about herself? Maybe she seemed confident on the outside, but once you got to know her she was insecure and needy and got teary at the drop of a hat?

There had to be some reason she was dating a man who was fifteen years older than she, a man who clearly wasn't about to marry her or give her the babies she wanted. Sure, my dad was good-looking and successful, but he also juggled much younger girlfriends far and wide, including one or two in Europe, to visit when he gave talks abroad. "One girlfriend, or three," he told me once. "But *never two*. If you have two, they'll find out about each other, and they'll be *pissed*."

This was the sort of pragmatic advice my father bestowed: advice that made no sense (*three* girlfriends wouldn't find out about one another somehow?), advice that had nothing to do with me.

My mother was even less helpful, limiting her counsel to some vague assertion of my obvious appeal as a person, while inevitably managing to cast a shadow of doubt on that appeal along the way. When I had a problem with a boyfriend and needed her input, her response was, "Who cares? If *he's* not interested, I'm sure someone better will come along as soon as he's gone."

"Who said he's not interested?"

"I'm not saying *that*, okay? I'm just saying it's *irrelevant*. You'll *always* have men eating out of your hands, no matter what you do. Why bother with someone who's lukewarm?"

"Who said he's lukewarm? Is that your impression?"

"Heather! *Jesus!* I'm just saying, there will always be lots of men who are interested in you, so why get hung up on someone who's on the fence?"

And so it went. Any practical discussion of whether this *particular* boyfriend was on the fence or not was out of the question. It didn't matter how much I said I liked him, or how much I wanted it to work. It was *beneath* my mother to mull whether this or that guy liked me or not, and it was beneath *me*, too. Why couldn't I see that? She preferred to look at the big picture—I was a catch, damn it!—and ignore the little day-to-day bumps in the road. She wished I would hurry up and learn to do the same thing.

My dad preferred the big picture, too. "All men are assholes!" he'd announce, almost gleefully. "Never forget that."

"*You're* a man."

"Yep. That's how I know."

But instead of looking at the big picture, instead of casting a suspicious eye on the guys around me, instead of *knowing* that for every lukewarm asshole in my sights, there was another asshole waiting in the wings to take his place, I wondered suddenly if I shouldn't nail down *one particular asshole* as soon as humanly possible.

After all, to hear Alice tell it, while college was a fertile paradise, teeming with young, virile men anxious to settle down and start earning money to support their beautiful wives and darling babies, postcollege life was a barren wasteland, populated by drunk losers and lecherous middle-aged divorcés who won't so much as let you borrow a bus pass after a night of hot sex.

So in keeping with Alice's very practical advice—the only practical, specific advice I'd probably ever received about love in the first nineteen years of my life—I spent the next fifteen years hoping to marry *every single guy I dated.*

I wanted to marry the hot, ambitious, but slightly shallow wannabe yuppie who knew way too much about expensive wine for a twenty-one-year-old. I wanted to marry the eccentric, stubbornly childlike aspiring filmmaker who thought marriage was a bourgeois trap designed to damn otherwise creative, spontaneous people to lives of mediocrity and silent longing. I wanted to marry the older divorcé who lounged around the house in MC Hammer pants, quoting his favorite passages from *Conversations with God.* I wanted to marry the balding, slightly overweight, perpetually unemployed stoner who had a life-size cut-out of the Emperor from *The Empire Strikes Back* in his bedroom.

Instead of assuming that there would always be attractive, interesting men around, I adopted Alice's scarcity mentality. I stretched out each relationship well past its natural shelf life. I remained committed despite big flaws and dysfunctional tics and major incompatibilities.

Even so, like the school principal who's determined to stick with even the hardest cases, I had impossibly high standards of behavior. I tried each boyfriend's patience to no end. I was faultfinding and relentless: *This is not how the man I'm going to marry should act!* I'd try to redirect his behavior, using polite but explicit terms. Hmm. How do I let him know that *the things I say should fascinate and intrigue my future husband*? How can I inform him, nicely, that my future husband should not talk about the wine at great length, or say things like *"My mama didn't raise no dummies— except for me and my brother!"* or wear MC Hammer pants? How can I make it clear that my future husband should mention how pretty I am, much, much more often? How can I make it obvious that my future husband is sure to ask about my day, then listen like his life depends on it?

Every step of the way, even as I was dumbfounded by how these men fell short, I never realistically evaluated our essential differences or made a rational assessment of our very obvious inability to move forward together, as a pair. With each guy, I thought that it was my one last chance to nab a husband before I lost my looks or resorted to dating middle-aged swingers. I just *had* to make this one work, there was no other option.

THE IRONY WAS THAT, right before Alice delivered her little speech, I had just broken up with the perfect guy, the ultimate future husband in all the world. Henry and I fell in love the first day of college. We stayed up late every night, talking and listening to REM and kissing and marveling over how perfect we were for each other. He was unbelievably cute and nice and crazy about me. He hung on my every word. He couldn't *wait* for his parents to meet me. He raved about how smart I was, how beautiful I was, how funny I was, how much he wanted to spend the rest of his life with me.

On Valentine's Day, he got me a huge heart-shaped box of chocolates, a necklace, a teddy bear, a heart-shaped balloon, and a dozen roses with a card that said: "This is what it's all about."

Even though I wanted to be caught up in the moment, I couldn't control the skeptical thoughts in my head. "Really?"

I thought. "*This* is what it's all about? *Valentine's Day?* It's all about buying a bunch of red crap for your girlfriend on a manufactured consumer holiday?"

But Henry was a romantic. He could get whipped into a state of almost hysterical sentimentality over any little thing: a walk through campus, a trip to our favorite BBQ joint, you name it. There was music playing in his head. He was at the center of his own little romance novel, and I was the ravishing lead with the flowing hair and heaving bosoms spilling out of her bustier.

College life isn't kind to romantics. That spring, as I reveled in the joys of drinking cold beer with rooms full of cute, flirtatious upperclassmen with broad shoulders and deep voices, Henry confessed that he sometimes worried that I would get bored and break up with him, sooner or later. I knew just what to say. "No, no, that'll never happen! That's so sweet that you're worried, though."

But I thought, "I'm going to get bored and break up with him, sooner or later."

And that fall, just as Henry had predicted, I fell in love with a tall, mercurial oddball named Finn. Finn would ramble on about highly personal stuff whenever he got drunk (which was often)—his relationship with his father, his ongoing existential crisis. He was smart and very intense and could talk for several hours straight, always viewing the world in alienated, suspicious terms. He was funny but he seemed a little depressed and whenever he sobered up, he couldn't remember any of our conversations. In other words, he was the perfect antidote to my somewhat clingy, oversensitive, hopelessly romantic boyfriend.

I became obsessed with Finn. How could I resist? Henry was

totally dedicated to me. Finn barely even recognized me. Henry wanted to spend the rest of his life with me. Finn was liable to pass out or wander home with some other girl at any second. Henry listened to my every word with great concentration and focus. Finn could hardly focus on my face when he was drunk, and didn't seem to know me at all the next day. What could be better?

So I dumped my perfect boyfriend. Henry was depressed for months. He wandered the hallways of his dorm at night, weeping audibly, keeping all of his friends awake.

The breakup was tougher for me than I expected. I missed Henry, and didn't realize how much I'd derived my happiness and confidence from his presence. There was only one thing to do to handle this loss: follow Finn around until he agreed to go out with me.

Eventually, Finn and I made out one night when we'd both been drinking, and soon we were "hanging out" regularly, although not officially dating. There were no flowers on Valentine's Day, no cards in which Finn called me his *best friend always and forever*, no mix tapes with sentimental titles featuring sappy songs by Don Henley, no long phone calls. I just showed up where I knew Finn would be, and at the end of the night, he rambled on about himself as we walked to my dorm room together.

And unlike Henry, who worried loudly over my tone of voice or what that look on my face meant, Finn hardly even noticed that I had a face. But he refused to discuss whether or not he was lukewarm or on the fence about me—this talk was beneath him. He had bigger, more existentially pressing fish to fry—just like my mother did! When he woke up, hungover, and saw his pale face in the mirror, he referred to himself as an asshole—just what my dad would've called him! In other words, while Henry felt unnaturally positive and warm and cloying, Finn felt *like home*.

Plus, he was really tall and he didn't listen to Don Henley.

This is how your mind works when you're nineteen years old. But once I had that awful conversation with Alice, I was tortured, because, well, *why was my future husband getting wasted and puking into that trash can, then flirting with a random woman he just met by the keg?*

Even so, this pattern continued for years. I rejected relationships with stable, genuinely interested men to go out with lukewarm, inappropriate, unavailable, self-involved, off-kilter mutants.

It would be unfair to call them assholes. Most of them were really nice guys, guys who could very easily make a less demanding, less impatient woman very happy, guys whom I made pay dearly for their future-husband status. And even as they pulled away, I became more determined to imitate what I thought a fulfilling relationship should look like: I prattled on endlessly about the farthest reaches of my emotional landscape, analyzing and unpacking past experiences, unleashing a torrent of what I thought were hopelessly charming anecdotes, escaping into rambling monologues on the unacceptability of patchy facial hair or pug dogs or insupportable fashion trends. I figured I deserved to loom large, to confess every detail of my history, to tell them absolutely *everything*. I thought I should be accepted and embraced for everything I felt and thought, for everything I'd ever felt and thought before. I figured I should be celebrated and honored and adored, like some kind of a demigod.

In other words, I was a lukewarm, inappropriate, unavailable, self-involved, off-kilter mutant. Maybe this was the glue, the common ground that kept me and my so-called future husbands together.

Yet, inevitably, each future husband would decide that he would prefer *not* to be my future husband. This took a longer period of time than you might imagine—somewhere between eighteen months and two years in most cases. Often, I was forced to end the relationship myself, but not without provocation: Typically my future husband had proclaimed his complete and total unwillingness to be my future husband several times before I finally relieved him of his duties.

This pattern finally shifted the night that my last so-called future husband, Dave, returned home from a trip to the East Coast and regaled me over an expensive welcome-back dinner (I was buying, of course) with tales of how he explained to *several* of his friends (and their happy, baby-flanked wives) that I was *very anxious* to get married, and that I had become despondent when I didn't get an engagement ring for my birthday. He related this story to me cheerfully and matter-of-factly, munching away at his dinner the whole time.

The humiliation! Of course he was right. I'd wanted an engagement ring for as long as I could remember—from *anyone*, really—but that's not what had made me so upset on my birthday. I'd been annoyed because he ran out to the drugstore that morning and returned with a copy of *Finding Nemo* (because he *loved* that movie!) and then asked me for some wrapping paper to wrap it with. *That was not how my future husband should act,* was all.

But this revelation really took the cake. Here was my future husband, a man who not only got me a crappy animated movie for my birthday, but who then told *everyone* that what I had *really* wanted was a ring! How deeply unacceptable! How . . . how demeaning!

"So . . ." I asked, willing myself not to lose my cool right there in the restaurant. "What did Ellen and Ava and Rebecca say?" I needed to know what the wives, with the babies on their hips and the adorable toddlers running around in their four-bedroom houses, had to say about all of this.

"They said you should dump me," not-my-future-husband blithely replied, stuffing his mouth full of fish.

I looked down at the untouched salmon on my plate, and suddenly it dawned on me: This was not how my future husband would act because *this was not my future husband!* This was just some balding, unemployed comedy writer, eating a good dinner on my dime. Hot damn, what was I even doing having *dinner* with this guy?

But I didn't say another word. I got up and walked out of the restaurant, and sat down by a fountain outside. It was time to take the very practical advice offered by these wives, albeit secondhand. It was time to look at the big picture. I was thirty-four years old. *I would always have men eating out of my hands,* I told myself. I tried to picture myself at sixty-five, old and gray, surrounded by fawning men.

Dave came out and sat next to me, smoking a cigarette, and I told him that he should move out. He finished his cigarette, and we went back inside and finished dinner.

I wish the story ended there, with me the picture of grace and self-restraint, silently moving forward alone, but that's not my style. After a few glasses of wine at the restaurant, we returned to the house we shared and I cried for at least an hour, blowing my nose loudly several times, and then, surrounded by a pile of snotty tissues, proceeded to deliver a series of lengthy treatises on my utter desirability as a future wife, including some extended musing on the totally unthinkable, insane notion that *anyone*, let alone *someone with a full-size cut-out of the Emperor in his bedroom* would *willfully* turn his back on the prospect of marrying me, glorious me, wonderful me, hot mustard and me, me!

Let's face it, if you have to expound upon your countless qualities as a future wife, you might as well just staple bologna to your face and screech like a wild bird. Making a strong case to a man about your viability as a prospective wife is about as wise as informing your current girlfriend that you know that she's going to dump you, sooner or later. I think that's what my mom was trying to tell me, years before, but somehow it took me twenty years to finally get it.

WHEN I KICKED DAVE OUT, I was Alice's age. Was there something wrong with me?

Yes. I was attracted to indifference. I settled, and then tortured my boyfriends for making me settle.

At age thirty-four, it was way too late to find someone *early*, as Alice had strongly recommended. I figured it was probably too late to find someone at all. I decided I would just have to adopt a baby on my own eventually. In the meantime, I'd get a few more dogs. I would work on my songwriting. I would write a novel or two. I would paint the rooms of my house weird colors. I would be messy and odd and interesting, the sort of woman who didn't worry about what men thought, at long last. I'd be the sort of woman who knew that men would *always* be interested in her, but didn't particularly care either way.

This dog-lady vision was comforting to me, somehow. And soon, instead of telling men I met that I was the perfect catch, I started to tell them the truth, based on what my ex-boyfriends had told me over the years: Like Alice, I was reasonably attractive, smart, opinionated, and anything but boring, but I was also very demanding and way too bossy and I went on and on about myself sometimes. Furthermore, despite appearances, I was insecure and needy and got teary at the drop of a hat.

That fall, I met a funny, smart professor. He was thoughtful and weird and talkative and sweet. Even though I was tempted to gloss over my flaws a little, I told him the truth. I warned him that I was impatient and demanding and emotionally overwrought and sentimental and earnest and exasperating, and I could be a serious pain in the ass.

"So, in other words, you're a woman," he said.

And I thought, *That's exactly what my future husband would say!*

14

The Flood Museum

When you walk into the Johnstown Flood Museum in Johnstown, Pennsylvania, the first thing you see is an uprooted tree, jutting into the center of the lobby, with a panicked-looking flood victim clinging to it for dear life. My father called me from his mother's house right after he'd seen it for the first time, to describe it in giddy detail. "It's incredible!" he gushed. "Around the lobby, there are all these little red buttons. When you press them, you hear water rushing, and people screaming!"

Sure, he was thrilled to see that the event that put his hometown on the map—the Johnstown Flood of 1889, which locals referred to as "The Great Flood"—had found such a fancy home. But more than that, he was captivated by the unabashedly morbid flavor of what he found there. Along with telling the story of that day, which his parents had described to him when he was a little kid, and which he had in turn described to me, the museum embraced a rubbernecker's appetite for the macabre—

otherwise surely someone would've said, *Look, do we really need a mannequin struggling against death in the middle of the lobby?*

Of course, my dad particularly loved any calamity that was caused by the arrogance and hubris of rich people. Having grown up in the working-class neighborhoods of Johnstown, where he returned home to his mother every night after playing all day, covered from head to toe in black soot from the nearby steel mills, he relished telling us how the richest industrialists in America, the Fricks and the Carnegies, summered by the shores of Lake Conemaugh, up the hill from Johnstown, but they didn't build their dam well enough. "The people downstream said, '*Fix the dam!*'" he'd say. "But those wealthy aristocrats, those captains of industry and robber barons, they just *laughed* and *ordered more martinis!* Then a big storm came, it rained and rained and the waters rose and rose. The heartless capitalists were warned again and again, but they just gossiped idly about their brand-new railroads and factories!

"Finally, the dam broke and a massive wall of water slammed down the mountain, crushing houses and drowning thousands of poor people in its path! A tower of water half a mile wide, filled with houses and bridges and barns and animals and people, hit Johnstown with the force of Niagara Falls!"

This was the stuff of bedtime stories, as far as my dad was concerned, a sweet little fairy tale about the catastrophic consequences of unchecked economic disparity in the world. He was a Marxist as an econ grad student, after all, bent on righting the wrongs of high capitalism and helping the poor people he'd grown up with, people who had no voice, who were doomed to be crushed by a wall of rushing water and debris, over and over again, thanks to the indifference of the rich and powerful.

Eventually, though, Milton Friedman lured my dad over to the dark side, or maybe Friedman just seemed like a survivor compared with Marx. My dad cared about justice, sure, but he cared about survival more. And let's face it, as much as you might mourn the men and women and children who drowned instantly that day in late May when the South Fork dam collapsed, your heart stayed with that one wild-eyed guy, clinging to the uprooted tree, determined not to go down with the rest of them.

"I DON'T LIKE THIS. I don't like this." My father is sitting up straight in his airplane seat, clenching his jaw, as if a dentist is wielding a drill right next to his face. He and I are flying to visit his parents, but we've been circling the airport in Pittsburgh for almost an hour, trying to land in the middle of a thunderstorm. The black clouds outside my window part only occasionally to reveal other planes, circling in the violent soup, lightning flashing in the windows, thunder rumbling through our bones. The plane buffets around in the wind, sometimes dropping fifty or sixty feet at a time while all those on board gasp and then hold their breath, each second of free fall experienced as a collective, desperate, silent prayer.

My heart is beating way too fast, my hands are sweating profusely, I clutch my dad's wrist on the armrest between us without thinking. But he isn't nearly as comforting as a dad should be, as far as I'm concerned. I'm nineteen years old, but I still want him to say, "Don't worry, honey." Something fatherly. He just sits there, rigidly, his head glued to his headrest, his jaw set in fear.

My dad might be fascinated by big disasters, but he isn't exactly brave. But then, morbid fixations really come in two varieties. There's the somewhat naive obsession with death favored by depressed teens, Goths, death-metal devotees, horror-movie fanatics, and Morrissey fans. These types relish death mostly as a forbidden cultural frontier, a sort of antidote to the upbeat, unthinking cheer of American culture. Death is just the ultimate affront to good taste, the kind of thing that instantly makes a room full of perky frauds uncomfortable.

But for a middle-aged man whose earliest memories are of a country caught in the ruthless grasp of World War II, a man who was diagnosed with high blood pressure in his mid-twenties, death is a fearsome reality that lingers on the edges of every picture. For my dad, focusing on big tragedies—the Johnstown Flood, the sinking of the *Titanic*, the Holocaust—is an act of reckoning, a way to let a little of the random, merciless nature of death into his life, to remind himself how lucky he is to be alive. Or maybe it's a matter of respect: By bowing down to the Grim Reaper's awesome powers, my father might somehow keep death's shadow from his door.

Flying in a plane is not a casual act for him, even though he flies overseas several times a year. Boarding a plane, for my father, is like drawing a line in the sand and inviting God to cross it.

Even so, when we're finally diverted to Cleveland and we've landed safely on the ground, my dad and I are already playing it off, trying to act like we didn't spend the last hour panicking and bargaining with God.

Luckily, my dad overhears the pilot telling another passenger that those were the worst conditions he's flown in in twenty years. We both feel vindicated for sweating and shaking in such a cowardly fashion. And to my dad's credit, when we debate whether to stay on the plane, which will fly back to Pittsburgh once the bad weather has passed, or rent a car and drive several hours in the dark instead, he rationally endorses flying, reasoning that it's far more dangerous to drive in the dark, in the rain, than it is to fly in after the storm blows through.

Still, we aren't completely relaxed until we're sitting at my grandmother's table in Johnstown with a big plate of homemade pierogi and a fork set in front of each of us. "Heather was gripping my arm so hard that it hurt!" my dad tells my grandfather.

"Oh yeah? Your whole face was sweating, and all you kept saying was, 'I don't like this. I don't like this.'" It must be strange for the Grim Reaper to see how much terror and respect he can elicit one minute, only to become a casual punch line the next, as if he were never there at all.

"Those planes aren't safe," offers my grandmother. "Huff won't even get on one. He refuses to fly."

"What, are you kidding?" my grandfather growled as he rolled another cigarette. "You'd have to have a death wish."

FOUR YEARS LATER, my dad and I are traveling to Johnstown together again, this time for my grandfather's funeral. He had had a stroke in his sleep a few days earlier. My grandmother, who's cut from stoical Russian stock, asserts that, in your late seventies, when you smoke and refuse to see a doctor, this isn't such a bad way to go. Short and sweet, no long good-byes.

No one on the Havrilesky side is fond of long good-byes. Long good-byes mean dealing with hospitals and crazy doctors and, worst of all, being forced to talk about your feelings—which is just uncomfortable and should really be avoided at all costs.

My dad and I board a tiny plane in Pittsburgh that will take us the last leg of our trip to Johnstown. We both hate tiny planes, so much that neither one of us says a single word about how horribly small this plane is, or how it only has five rows, with just two seats on each row. But when we hit our first big cloud, we both let out a deep, worried sigh at the same time. It feels like we're bumping through the sky in a minivan.

I really don't want to be here, on this plane. I feel like we're tempting fate, flying together again after our last awful trip. Plus, I hate funerals and I don't want to contemplate my grand-father's death or see any sad family members or anything like that. I'm twenty-three years old, possibly at my personal peak of immaturity and irresponsibility and cynicism. I want to be back in San Francisco, getting drunk with my friends.

But I knew, when my dad called me to tell me the news, that my brother and sister would never go to the funeral. Eric is in Los Angeles and has a demanding job, and Laura is busy with med school. I knew my dad would feel ashamed if he didn't have at least one kid with him at the funeral. I couldn't let him show up without one kid. That seemed unfair. And he knew I was the most likely candidate. I could hear it in his voice over the phone. He *needed* me to go with him.

It's strange, when you realize that your parents need you in ways they won't say. But I don't want to think about that right now. I'm happy to let it pass without comment, just as I'm determined not to discuss our obvious mutual fear of flying while we're still in the air.

But as we're getting close to the very small mountaintop airport in Johnstown, the pilot announces to the four of us on the plane, "We'll be arriving in *John Town* in about ten minutes."

My stomach lurches. I pray that my dad won't openly acknowledge what we both heard.

No such luck. "Did you hear that?" my father gasps, full-on panic in his voice. "He said John Town. John Town! He's never flown here before! We're about to land at a tiny airport, on a mountaintop, in the fog, and *he's never even flown here before!*"

Sure enough, the plane misses the runway on the first try. We have to circle back and try again. My mind is racing. Can this plane do an instrument landing, or is it too small to have equipment like that on board? If it doesn't have that stuff, does that mean we have to rely on the pilot's vision? I look down and can't see a thing but low clouds. I strain to see something, anything. There, the top of a tree! We're only thirty feet up, at the most! My heart races. My hands are soaked. My dad gulps loudly and doesn't speak, grasping both armrests.

We hit the runway with a rattling crash and do a long, skittery, screeching slide that feels like the kind of dangerous scenario that might be described in amateur piloting handbooks. Finally, the pilot gains the upper hand and the plane gradually slows to a stop. We're on the ground. The mist is closing in around us. I feel faint.

When we step off the plane and across the tarmac, I tell my dad I need to lie down for a minute on the rug in the tiny airport lobby. My dad chuckles and says, "You look as white as a ghost."

Then he stops laughing. "I feel sort of sick, too."

At the wake, my grandfather's body lies in an open casket at the front of a room full of relatives, old friends, and neighbors. A group of older women with hair dyed jet black and rosaries in their hands are kneeling in front of the casket, reciting one Hail Mary after another with an odd, uniform intonation that reminds me of Mike Ditka. These are the "prayer ladies," my grandmother explains in a whisper when I take a seat next to her. They go around, reciting the rosary at Catholic wakes all weekend long. I try to imagine them, kneeling in front of one rouged corpse after another, repeating the same singsong about *the fruit of thy womb, Jeee-sus!* Is this how they beat back the darkness, how they keep death at bay?

My grandmother, at least, seems like she's in pretty good spirits, under the circumstances. One of my cousins, on the other hand, looks ten years older than I instead of seven years younger, and she keeps saying she's coming down with something in a tone that makes me think she isn't used to going without some kind of pill or drug for such a long stretch. She describes her exciting life as a waitress in San Diego in the most glowing terms, but with a grim look on her face, as if our grandfather might sit up and grab her arm and pull her into his casket at any second.

I duck away from her as she pours her third or fourth styrofoam cup of coffee, and my aunt quickly introduces me to an old family friend, a shaking, fragile woman who clutches my hand

and blinks confusedly at me as I answer her questions about life in San Francisco.

Twenty minutes later, the woman collapses at the front of the chapel and she's taken off in an ambulance.

"The excitement gets to these old people, and it's too much for them," my dad tells me as we're pulling up to his father's gravesite. The casket is waiting there, ready to be lowered into the ground forever.

"Don't do any of this shit for me," he whispers in my ear. "Cremation, that's it. I don't want any of this shit."

That night we get a call and find out that the frail, shaking woman I spoke with at the wake died at the hospital that afternoon. "That happens all the time," my grandmother assures us in a breezy tone, as if she and thousands of others just like her are already well on their way, drifting off this earthly plane like a big bundle of helium balloons released at a football game, floating off to meet the mother of God and the fruit of her womb, Jeeesus. It happens all the time. Just wave good-bye and move on.

THREE YEARS LATER, I'm at my dad's gravesite, watching an obscenely overpriced casket sink into the ground, covered in a cascade of white roses. *You have to understand*, I tell my dad as the casket disappears below ground level. *Look at your mother. If we had you cremated, she'd be sure your soul was going to hell.* That's what my mom had said, anyway. She said my dad would've done whatever his mother wanted, if he knew his mother would still be alive when he died.

But Christ, look at this circus, my dad says. *Is Wendy here? Did she meet the other one yet?*

Yeah . . . she's figuring it out. She said there was some girl hanging around, and everyone seemed to know her. She showed up for a gathering at Divine's last night.

This makes my dad laugh. Why not? He's free. Free from the madness, finally. Like we sang in chorus once: *Great God, Almighty, I am free at last!* No reason to keep hurtling forward, ahead of that crushing wall of water. Free to wander through like a tourist, take in the sights, and leave whenever you want. Three current girlfriends and four ex-girlfriends at the funeral, with one of the girlfriends claiming that he'd proposed just the day before, and nothing to show for it but a bedroom set. *We told her to take anything she wanted from the condo.* My dad is hardly listening now, distracted by the sight of so many old friends, gathered in one place. A tisket, a tasket, a five-thousand-dollar oak casket! But why should he care? These are our petty concerns, not his.

He did get a good laugh when his former student stood up at the funeral and recounted how my dad had told his entire class not to become doctors or lawyers like their parents had instructed them to. She said he made them all look out the window, and he pointed to Duke Chapel outside. "Major in that!" he'd said. "Major in *that!*" The student believed this meant that they should *major in life*, that they should seize the day and follow their true calling.

But my dad literally meant that they should go to Divinity School. He had urged me to do the same a few years earlier. We need more philosophers and spiritual guides, and fewer money-

lenders in the temple, he said. His advice always was a little eso-
teric, particularly for an economist.

But wasn't he right? Wasn't it prescient, his obsession with
big, pressing questions? Even when he was juggling three girlfriends and polishing off a good bottle of red wine every night,
he was always preoccupied with the big picture. Some people
just exude an existential desperation, a feeling that time is running out, that something is chasing them down, ready to strike.
Like his fear of flying, this wasn't a fixation he mentioned often, but clues of it were everywhere: in the way he gave advice, like he might not be around to tell you this again, in the
solemn voice of Billie Holiday mourning some lost love on his
stereo, in the books on his shelves, which either concerned the
darkest turns of history from the Great Depression to Watergate,
or had titles like *Centering: A Guide to Inner Growth*, or *The Only
Dance There Is.*

Not that he didn't have a sense of humor about the whole
thing. How could you miss the humor in it, the glorious, stupid
wrath on us all? We live for a while and die unexpectedly, without warning.

Of course, my father had plenty of warnings. He was starting
to get chest pains when he ran in the morning, chest pains he
mentioned to me when we ran together the last time I saw him,
two months earlier in San Francisco. I told him that didn't sound
good at all, that he should call his doctor when he got home. I
stupidly didn't tell my sister, who's a doctor and would've driven
him to the emergency room on the spot. He didn't tell my sister,
either. He may not even have told his doctor when he went in
for a checkup one month later.

Did he think of death all those years, only to refuse to save his own life? Was I supposed to insist, was I supposed to call Laura myself? I was too young and dumb to follow up. For all of my fears, I thought we would all live forever. I never thought he would have to fight to survive, that we all would.

The organ played the Duke fight song. *Fight, we'll fight, with all our strength and might!* The minister was hesitant to allow the song, questioning its appropriateness in a place of worship. But he finally gave in after Eric, who rarely speaks up in such situations, explained that it was a fitting tribute to our father, assuring the pastor that it would sound quite *regal* when played on the organ, in a sacred setting. He didn't mention the fact that Duke fans typically yell "Eat shit!" at the end of one of the verses.

Eat shit! yelled my dad when the organ got to that part. *Eat shit!* he yelled, to drown out the sound of sniffling children, sniffling friends and ex-girlfriends. It must feel good, to stand clear of the confusion and the wreckage at last, to float above it, amused instead of heartbroken. It must feel good, to be detached from the turmoil and the anguish of it all, at long last.

Eat shit! he yells at me in the mornings as I run through our old neighborhood, over the warped sidewalks, under the giant oak trees. But he can imagine just how good it feels to breathe the hot, moist Durham air, in and out, like he used to. It's okay to miss him, but he doesn't want me to feel bad for him. He wants me to relish how good it is to be alive, how lucky I am. I will savor this life, I think, I will stop wasting my time with dumb guys and crappy jobs that lead nowhere. I will be bold. I will throw myself into life instead of hiding from it, I will cast aside this constant suspicion that something big and scary is waiting for me around every corner.

Because there *is* something big and scary waiting, it's there and it will never go away. "We've all got a death sentence on our heads," my dad's brother tells me breezily when he arrives at our front door the day before the funeral, as if he's a neighbor stopping by for a casual visit on his way to the grocery store. Long good-byes are not my uncle's style. "We're all going to die, I hate to break it to you," he says with a smile, in a tone that's a little soothing and a little aggravating at the same time.

He's right, of course. But miraculously enough, there is still strong coffee and there are still doughnuts. There are raindrops and close friends. Everything crashes down around you, but it really is as hilarious as it is sad, just like the Flood Museum. *The cheap caskets looked like those vinyl faux-wood tables at McDonald's! I* tell my dad one morning. *The undertaker passed out tissues and said professionally soothing things! I* tell him. *We almost dressed you in your peach-colored Larry loafers!*

Most of the day, I can't live with this tragedy. But every now and then, it feels like something my dad himself has actively chosen, to avoid the slower, far less tolerable torment of old age. Maybe my dad is in on the joke and he loves it, the whole ugly mess he left behind.

Or maybe not. Maybe he simply exited without a long good-bye. But the rest of us don't really have a choice, the long good-bye goes on and on. I say good-bye to him every morning and every night of my life. Sweet, dark, magnificent you, the kingdom, and the power, and the glory are yours, forever and ever. Good-bye, good-bye, good-bye.

I HAVEN'T BEEN BACK to my father's gravesite since his funeral. It feels disrespectful—not keeping away, but showing up there and staring at some plot of shaggy grass and red clay soil. It doesn't feel fair to reduce him to a little square of earth, a small engraved stone. It would anger him to see me there, summing up his bright, crazy existence with some numbers carved into a rock, defining his adventure as a tragedy just because it ended.

It looks like a tragedy, but it's actually a comedy. It looks like a catastrophe, but it's actually a call to action. He seems to be lost and gone forever, but maybe he's closer than he's ever been before.

Before now, I found this kind of thinking about dead people a little bit pathetic, just another frantic lie people tell themselves to ease the pain. I had no idea that sometimes, the stakes are so high that you have no choice. The stakes are so high that you're forced to come to some private conclusion. You cling to whatever it takes to make it through the day, whether it's an outright lie or a soothing half-truth, whether it's fifty Hail Marys or fifteen thousand Eat Shits. The death sentence is never lifted. The stakes are so high that there are no stakes at all; you might as well live like it's all just an elaborate dream.

Study that mannequin clinging to the wreckage, hoping to beat the odds. Push the red buttons to hear the screams, and picture the actors the museum hired to yell in agony over the sound of rushing water. We are all collaborators in one great big farce. Turn to your fellow actors and exchange a knowing smile. We are all in on the horror and the whimsy, we can all revel together in the foolishness, the richness, the emptiness, the loveliness of this beautiful mess.

One of the books I found on my father's shelves was *The Wisdom of Insecurity* by Alan Watts, a philosopher who majored in life and died of heart failure in his sleep at age fifty-eight. (My father died of heart failure in his sleep at age fifty-six.) In the book, Watts sums up the exquisite nothingness, the divine imperfection of the universe, by pointing to a poem by Edward Lear about the old man of Spithead who throws open his window and says,

Fill jomble, fill jumble,
Fill rumble-come-tumble.

In his nonsensical phrases, the old man invites the unknowns into his life, the tragic and the comic and the uplifting and the devastating and everything in between. Invite the good and the bad, with open arms: endings and beginnings, come-from-behind victories and lost loves, sunny afternoons and plane crashes, prayer ladies and junkies, funerals and fight songs. We are all clinging to some uprooted tree, being hurled down the rushing river. Of course it's not fair. We'll disappear, and soon we'll be forgotten. Free at last!

15

Disastrously Unprepared

Last week on the freeway, a car did a three-sixty and crashed into the shoulder, right in front of me. I pulled over and called 911, then got out of my car and walked back along the road to make sure the driver was okay. No one else had stopped.

A woman in her late twenties with dust all over her face was standing by her car, crying and shaking. I led her to my car, gave her a Handi-Wipe for her face, and listened as a torrent of panicked words flowed from her mouth—she was unemployed, she didn't have insurance, she shouldn't have been driving at all, people were so crazy on the freeway. I agreed that people were crazy. I told her that I saw the guy in the pickup cut right into the lane where she was. I told her that it wasn't her fault, that she was lucky she wasn't hurt, that the cops would come and they would fine her, not arrest her, for driving without insurance. When the tow truck came, I gave her my number in case she needed a witness. I gave her a hug and told her good luck.

The next day, when she found my number in her wallet, she

would remember me as the lady who stopped and remained calm at the scene of the accident. To her, I would be the woman with the two kids' car seats in her car, the kind of mature adult who stays clearheaded and calls 911 and then offers hugs and empathizes and has a travel pack of Handi-Wipes in her glove compartment.

What the hell has happened to me?

RIGHT BEFORE THE ACCIDENT, I was listening to Eckhart Tolle on my car stereo. He's the guy who tells you to *live in the now*—sort of like Ram Dass, but more clean cut, and with a German accent. "Please pay attention not just to the words, but to *the silent spaces between the words*," he was telling me as I hurtled down the freeway at seventy miles an hour. "*That's* where the shift happens." I was trying to focus on the silent spaces between the words as a means of putting my worries and neurotic thoughts aside. I wanted to shake off the frustrations of my workday before I picked up my daughter from day care. I wanted to be relaxed and present, not harried and distracted and bossy. I wanted to be *living in the now.*

I've turned into a crusty old cliché, in other words.

But I had the Eckhart Tolle on my car stereo only because, back when I was trying to gather the will to dump the last of a string of freewheeling, noncommittal stoner boyfriends, I was given the CD by a Reiki healer recommended by a friend who was having so much trouble *living in the now* that she could barely sleep at night. I was skeptical, but the Reiki healer, despite having a job title that sounds like an exotic dog breed, was a very good listener. Sure, she would conjure the spirits of the universe occasionally, rallying them to aid me in my quest to find myself and, if necessary, ditch the man whose childlike sense of wonder seemed to require him to remain unemployed indefinitely.

But the universe *did* seem to be on my side more often during that time, plus the healer gave very pragmatic advice: *Exercise. Get more sleep. Read this book. Stop thinking that way.* Mostly she encouraged me to open myself up to the unknown, to stop hiding from the world. She quickly recognized that I was a creature of habit, interested in safety above all else, and she could see how it compromised my enjoyment of life. She told me to try new things for a change, to drive to new places, to stop and eat at random Chinese restaurants and taco trucks, to wander through the world with open eyes, to dare to be vulnerable in the face of life's unpredictable twists and turns. I ate some really bad Chinese food during that time, but something shifted inside me. I became more courageous. I listened to the Eckhart Tolle CD she gave me only twice before I resolved to dump the stoner and move on.

Breaking up with him was easy, actually, compared with agonizing over our relationship for way too long. The only sad moment I had was when he carried his life-size cardboard replica of the Emperor from *Star Wars* out of my house forever: I knew I'd never go out with anyone quite like him again. This was both cause for celebration and a reason to mourn the end of an era. I would be free of this foot-dragging, overgrown child, yes, but I might never embark on a two-hour drive for a really good doughnut again.

Once I broke up with him, though, I had a sense that everything was going to work out for me. I was independent and strong, at last! I was open to the infinite possibilities of the universe!

I threw a big party. I lost ten pounds. I bought a really nice king-size bed and mattress for me and my dog, Potus, to share. And as I was painting the room that was once my boyfriend's office a defiantly girly shade of lavender pink, I thought: *This is the start of my new life! Everything will make sense from this point forward. I won't need therapists or healers or New Age CDs, ever again. I am open to the world, I am vulnerable, I am confident and strong. I will take whatever comes. I will live with the dangers of the world, I will lean into the chaos!*

I would be just like that calm Farrah Fawcett look-alike on the box of my parents' fire-escape ladder, the one that never left the closet: relaxed and confident under pressure, with a slight smile on my face, even as flames licked the hem of my nightgown.

THE BABY IS CRYING. The two-year-old won't put on her underwear. My husband left for an early meeting, so it's all up to me. The dogs need to be fed. The sink is filled with dirty dishes. And before he left for school, my thirteen-year-old stepson told us that if he has to spend another day in a room that's painted lavender pink, he's going to lose his mind.

The world is one big blaring alarm clock going off in my ear, but I'm staring blankly at myself in the mirror. My hair is pulled back in a knot—not the carefree knot of a younger woman who hit the bars last night, but the perpetual, frazzled-looking knot of a thirty-nine-year-old mother who spends her free minutes (what free minutes?) staring into the middle distance like a ghost, fantasizing about central air-conditioning. I look haggard and confused. *Why am I getting it all wrong?* Why can't I be the kind of mom who gets up early to work out, then showers and styles her hair and gets dressed, the kind of smooth professional who can jiggle the baby while coaxing the two-year-old into her underwear? Why can't I be the relaxed, organized career mom instead of some harried, slovenly zombie?

But I know the answer to that: I am not and was never going to be the relaxed, organized, manicured career mom, any more than I was going to be the shiny, effusive cheerleader or the diligent Gap employee or the virginal good girl or the wise young lady who dates only responsible, emotionally available guys. I am a disorganized, melancholy second-guesser who rhapsodizes a little too loudly over the pleasures of a cold beer at the end of a long day. I am enthusiastic, yes, and passionate, sure, but I'm also fundamentally ambivalent, angst-ridden, and conflicted. I am distracted, overwhelmed, and mostly unprepared for whatever lies ahead.

Sure, I was the lady with the Handi-Wipes who stayed calm and called 911, but tomorrow I might be the one with dust on her face, crying and panicking.

For the last five months since my second daughter was born, I've been running in circles through my house, whispering "Sweet Jesus" under my breath. My mind has been reeling at how much work it takes just to think straight, just to get some semblance of dinner together or to remember to pack some extra shirts for day care.

Having two very small kids means constantly marveling at how unprepared I am—for the noise, for the lack of sleep, for the constant work, for the level of service to which each child clearly feels entitled. In the midst of the storm, when everything is falling apart, I can't stop thinking, *Who can I pay to do all of this unpleasant work, all of this scrambling around, fixing breakfasts and pumping breast milk and vacuuming floors, so that I can relax and read books and think my own thoughts and gaze sweetly at the baby for a few hours, then go out and get fall-down drunk on margaritas with my friends?*

I am not the one who smiles ever so slightly as the world goes up in flames. I am not the one who faces challenges head-on, gets really organized, and *works smarter.* I'm not even the one who showers regularly.

I am the messy disaster, the daydreamer, the disheveled, self-deprecating deep sigher. I am the one who complains bitterly about twisted car-seat straps and an ungodly tide of dirty laundry that never seems to subside. I'm the one who snickers mirthlessly when a moth flies into the baby's milk and it all has to get poured down the sink.

But I'm not that worried about impending disasters anymore. I just want to know how other people my age with my responsibilities get by. I want to know how they try and fail, and I want to know *exactly* how they feel and act and what they say when they're failing.

"This is a *fucking clown show!*" is what one friend tells me he says when everything is going wrong. "What's a clown show?" I asked. He wasn't sure, but I think I know from my own experience: it's loud, stuff is spilling on the floor, and you can't all fit into the car.

But you could never fit into the car in the first place—that was only an illusion. You can do your best to accept your flaws and get a reasonable hold on your circumstances. But no one wakes up one day and suddenly they're *living in the now*—even the Reiki healer and Eckhart Tolle and the spiritual masters of the universe agree on that.

You're never fully prepared. You never really arrive. The best you can do is to keep painting the walls to suit your new circumstances.

AND THEN, just when I decide that I'll never get a handle on anything, it all comes together: I get a good haircut on Friday, and on Saturday I wake up early and run the dogs for three miles straight. I shower and put on earrings. I sit and read the paper while the baby is napping. I play in the baby pool with my two-year-old while my husband makes us all dinner, then I have a beer and watch Suze Orman yell at people who are far less financially responsible than I am, while the baby yells along from her play chair.

That's it! I think. *I've finally turned the corner!* Everything is *right.* I've arrived at last. Everything will be perfect *from now on!*

Of course that's not true. But this is: I love this fucking clown show of mine. The unruly dogs, the distracted husband, the alternately sweet and enraged two-year-old, the enormous baby who still wakes up at four a.m. even though she clearly has the fat stores to hibernate through a long winter. I love them all, along with my emotionally overwrought teenage stepson and my little, overheated house and my hairy rugs and my smudged windows and my scrappy, overgrown yard, and all of the imperfect manifestations of this imperfect life. I am flawed, flawed, flawed, and I will rarely feel shiny and complete and utterly calm and prepared.

And sure, while I'm at it, I will never be gorgeous and rich. I will never float across the spotless floors of my seaside mansion, humming to myself, as someone else prepares my children a gourmet lunch and walks the dogs and folds the clothes, quietly, so I am finally free to stare out the windows or, more likely, flip impatiently through magazines, hoping for something else.

See where perfection takes you? To a quiet, scentless prison, staffed by strangers. But there is no end point or final resting place, at least not while you're still alive. And no one is safe, not even the young and the beautiful, not even the hopelessly rich. Their money and their looks and their youth and their leisurely lives are not safe; we are all living on borrowed time, as thieves and old age and tedious work and natural disasters and the apocalypse loom at the edge of the picture, ready to blot us out, like ants, under an unforgiving thumb.

But look how *hard* we try, you and me, us and them, *everyone*. Isn't it sort of sweet, to see how determined we are to do better, to be stronger, to make sure our kids and our mothers and our partners and even our dogs know that they're loved? Sometimes, even as my world is in chaos, I see myself, braiding my daughter's hair, drinking my tea, blending up a fruit smoothie and singing and dancing crazily to distract the baby from the blender's scary, grinding sound, and I think: That woman is weird, but she does seem to be enjoying herself. That woman is a little bit of a wreck, but at least her kids seem to like her.

And I see *you*, too, sometimes, on the street and in the park and at the grocery store, you with your odd habits and your strange phone voice, you in your soft pants with your great big ideas and your deep sighs. You are just like me.

We are frazzled and unruly, you and me. We are desperate and wistful and restless and funny and frayed at the edges. We can worry that we're doing it all wrong, we can long for central air or true love or a view of the ocean, and that's just part of the fucking clown show. We can be ingrates and role models, we can be flinchy and heroic, we can be courageous and also melancholy. There is nothing wrong with feeling unsafe and uncertain. There is nothing wrong with addled, misguided parenting, or self-involved rambling. I give you permission, my friend, to continue on this twisted, sweet path of suffering and satisfaction and distraction. I give you my blessing, my partner in failing at everything. I am witness to your grace and your faltering. I give you my undying love, as you struggle and stutter and the sun falls from the sky.

When the earth stops spinning, we will panic. There is no avoiding it. We'll be crying and shaking, just like that woman at the side of the road, wondering if we did it the right way. We'll wonder if we failed ourselves, or failed each other, if we were a big disappointment, in the end.

Please remember, we were not a disappointment. Not at all, not even close. We were gorgeous and strong, you and me. We were terrible and troubled and utterly divine.

ACKNOWLEDGMENTS

Sincere thanks to the old-fashioned editor of my dreams, Megan Lynch, who nudged me to write a book and then patiently, painstakingly, helped me shape it. Thanks also to Sarah Bowlin, Geoff Kloske, and all the other great people at Riverhead. Thanks to Gary Morris, my literary agent, who has listened to my crappy ideas for twelve years without once hanging up abruptly like the agents on TV always do. Thanks to Kerry Lauerman, Sarah Hepola, Joan Walsh, and Laura Miller at Salon.com for their input and support. Thanks to Christina Askounis for her warmth and encouragement. For their friendship and patience over the decades, thanks to Kelly Atkins, Parker Lutz, Lara Frank, Andrea Russell, Stephen Lavine, Carina Chocano, and Apryl Lundsten. Thanks to my mother, Susan Havrilesky, an excellent story-teller and the most generous person I know, who read this book four times front to back and somehow tolerated the narrow perspective of its author. Thanks to Laura and Eric for their love, patience, games of Cousins, and tomato fizzes. Thanks to Claire, Ivy, and Zeke for putting up with me, and thanks most of all to Bill Sandoval, the most beautiful birthday princess in all the land.